CONTENTS

THANK GOODNESS THEY CAN'T TALK!

INTRODUCTION

Geoff, With A Little Help From Mouse, Reveals Their Long Kept Secrets

The dozens of stories in this book are not just about Geoff's unbelievable adventures, also they revolve around family, staff, cats, dogs, and their sometimes eccentric owners.

Geoff enlightens readers with secrets that the public never gets to hear. He brings the animals and the characters to life, making readers laugh out loud as they visualise some of the extraordinary events, coincidences, catastrophes, and near tragedies that take place.

Geoff started the business off in a small way, but it wasn't long before it became a very busy bustling establishment. Indeed, in the later years, it was not unusual for one hundred cats and two hundred dogs to pass through the premises on a busy August day which Chapter 8, Pure Unadulterated Mayhem reveals.

The first chapter gets off to a hilarious rip-roaring start. It is about a cute foxy-looking mongrel cross called Benson. Benson is a lovable but very devious character whom readers will love as he causes Geoff's blood pressure to rise to the core. And there are many more acts like him to follow.

Preceding each chapter is an outstanding rustic caricature giving a clue to the next chain of events, and Geoff would like to point out, that his nose is not that big.

Throughout the United Kingdom and the world, people love their pets, and when they take a vacation, they take meticulous care of where they board them.

But, did the owners know what kind of mischief their precious pets got up to?

Well, they had absolutely no idea.

As the title suggests, Thank goodness they can't talk!

Many a pet lover's dream is to own and run a pet boarding business, but after reading Geoff's long-kept secrets they might well have second thoughts...

SETTING THE SCENE

Please study the aerial view of Home Sweet Home because a lot of action takes place in this area, especially in the very first Chapter, CAN I TRUST HIM?

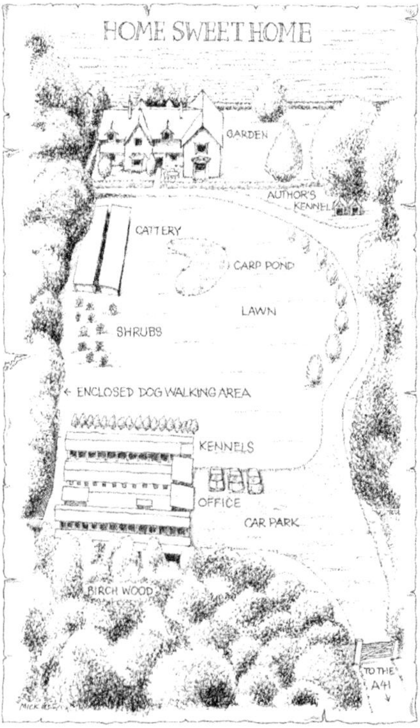

Previously, the one-hundred-and-fifty-year-old cottage known as Keepers Cottage was home to a long line of gamekeepers and I was the very last gamekeeper to reside there along with my wife Kathy.

Cattery

Here is a very early photo of the cattery. We opened before I had time to paint the ladders white. Residing are our first feline guests who are relaxed and waiting to be fed. Unfortunately, they get quite an unpredictable shock in the first hilarious Chapter.

Kennels

This is the original kennel block with the woodland in the background where we walked our canine guests twice daily. The woodland path is where a lot of the action takes place in the following stories.

Posing for the camera is Taz a Rottweiler, Dan a mongrel cross, Beauty a large black Labrador, (she features in the last hilarious chapter) Goldie, a lovely Golden Retriever and Albert a very placid English Bull Terrier.

CHAPTER 1

Can I Trust Him?

This is a story about a dog called Benson, the climax is so far-fetched it is hard to believe that it is true.

But unfortunately for me... It was!

At the beginning of my exciting new career, when I was working alone in our brand-new pet boarding business, the intake of cats and dogs took off very rapidly. It wasn't long before I had more than thirty dogs and twenty cats to look after. For one person, that is a heck of a lot of work. Kathy and I knew we would need an assistant or two soon, but I needed to manage on my own as long as possible. It meant we didn't have to start paying staff wages while we were repaying the small bank overdraft on the business.

Kathy's sister Ann lived with us for a while, and she was a great help, especially with the cats, as you will soon find out in this incredible story about Benson.

Kathy and Ann helped me in any way they

could. In the summer, we got up at 5 am each morning to walk the dogs before the two sisters went to their respective workplaces and before I was likely to receive any customer phone calls or customers arriving on the carpark. In the evenings, when the girls came home, we walked the dogs again, and as it was summertime, the long daylight hours were a bonus. In the beginning dog walking was a novelty, especially when we had friends over for an evening because they also helped to walk them. For sure, it was great fun and entertainment for everyone. In a later hilarious chapter, Ken, Kathy's brother did not find it fun at all.

The three of us walked the dogs around a circuit in the beautiful surrounding woodland, which consisted of oak, mountain ash, birch, and Scotch pine. The path that I had cut with a long straight-handled slashing knife wound through bright green bracken that had grown to about four feet high on either side. This made us feel totally alone in a beautiful tranquil world. When we were halfway through dog walking during the mornings and evenings, Ann's routine was to go down to the cattery, which was a couple of hundred yards away to feed the cats.

Take note, Anne's routine is very important information regarding this story.

Now here we come to my friend Benson.

Benson belonged to Donna, a friend of Kathy's from work. They both worked in the same department at Barclays Bank, Radbroke Hall near Knutsford in Cheshire. On most weekends, Donna boarded Benson in our kennels. She lived quite close to the bank's premises, and with it being over fifty miles away from our establishment, it made good sense for Kathy to bring Benson back with her on a Friday evening and then take him back to Cheshire the following Monday morning. Both Donna and Kathy worked away in London a lot, so Benson had many seven-day stays with us.

Benson was a mongrel, and for sure, there is nothing wrong with mongrels because they are often more intelligent and smarter than the purest of breeds. And he certainly fitted into the smart category. In fact, he turned out to be downright devious. Benson was a little bit smaller than a Labrador and a similar colour to a fox. He had a very adorable, mischievous face with large black eyebrows that made him look more like a playful human being than a dog. Benson was just over a year old and was full of life and energy, just as he should have been for a dog of that age. He became a real pal of mine, and it was only natural that the three of us, Kathy, Ann, and myself, wanted to walk our favourite dogs.

So, I always chose to walk my favourite, my best mate Benson.

Benson was very friendly with other dogs, especially bitches, and he never showed any sign of aggression to any of the male dogs that boarded with us. All the dogs that came to our kennels had to be fully vaccinated, so it was never a problem to walk some of them together, providing they liked each other of course. Benson usually had the pleasure of walking with one or sometimes two bitches. With Benson boarding with us so frequently, he got to know the premises and other dogs really well, but more importantly, he knew the dog walking routine inside out.

Benson knew he was my favourite, and when I was walking him, he used to look up at me with his appealing mischievous big brown eyes as if to say,

"Come on Geoff, let me off the lead. I know this place like the back of my paws."

My strict rule was, WE DO NOT let someone else's dog off the lead unless you know you can outrun it, and as fit and fast as I was, I knew that there was no chance of me ever outrunning Benson. I saw Benson so often, I felt that I was his owner and I would like to believe that he thought the same.

One day, just as we were about to start the morning's dog walking session, Kathy, Ann and me stood by Benson's kennel discussing if we should try letting him off the lead or not. Benson was looking at us from one to the other with an imploring look on his face, just as if he knew that we were discussing him. I am sure that if he could have talked, he would be saying YES, YES, YES.

Well, because of Benson's irresistible pleading looks, he was going to get his way. He was going to be set free.

Our plan was, I was going to take Benson out with two other dogs into the wood and let him off enabling me to walk the other two comfortably, and trust him to exercise himself with a little supervision from the three of us as we all walked the circuit at the same time.

This new idea worked successfully for many weeks. Benson thoroughly enjoyed himself, and so did we. He appeared completely trustworthy as he obediently came back every time I called. In his excitement he ran round the circuit several times to our one and looked to be moving at a hundred miles an hour. Each time Benson passed the dogs I was walking, he appeared to be showing off and glared at them with a human-like self-gratifying smirk on his face. I found it quite amusing to think that he was trying to make the other dogs jealous.

Little did I realise that my amusement was not going to last!

As everyone knows, things do not always go to plan, and as I should have suspected.

The inevitable happened...

One sunny morning, I was walking two black Labrador bitches with Benson on the loose, zooming around the circuit as per usual. Blackbirds and song thrushes were singing, wrens chattering, and I was whistling a Beatles tune. The calming atmosphere put me in a carefree mood. I felt like I was floating on a sea of tranquility. My mate Benson had done about four of his daily twenty laps.

But, after about five minutes of not seeing him, it

suddenly dawned on me.

Where on earth is he?

It usually took Benson about two and a half minutes to do his circuit while seemingly grinning at all the other dogs on their leads as he shot past them.

After another five minutes of no Benson, I shouted to Kathy, who was somewhere on the other side of the tall bracken,

"KATHY, HAVE YOU SEEN BENSON?"

She shouted,

"HE SHOT PAST ME ABOUT FIVE MINUTES AGO. I THOUGHT HE WAS WITH YOU?"

I was not unduly worried and thought he would probably turn up in a few minutes. Perhaps he was sniffing around and marking his territory with numerous leg cockings and peeing as male dogs often do.

But still no Benson!

I realised that he had been missing for over ten minutes, and the speeds he could achieve meant he could be miles away.

'NO, NO, NO, not my Benson. You wouldn't do this to me. Surely you wouldn't, you little devil!'

'Oh yes, he would and he has.'

I could have used some powerful language that for sure was not for sensitive ears. My so-called mate Benson had been conning me all the time, making me believe that I could trust him. I had a horrible feeling my sea of tranquility was going to turn into a...TSUNAMI!

When Benson disappeared that morning, the two black Labradors I was walking were sisters, so I decided to keep them with me to entice him near enough for me to grab him. I knew he liked the two good-looking young ladies because he had been out with them on numerous walks. He always had an admiring glint in his eyes. Admiring glint is a keyword to this story! So, hopefully, when I called him, he would run back to see me and, of course, my two silky black companions.

I thought that was an excellent plan.

So, leading the two black beauties I hurried from the woodland back into our grounds. I spotted the bad boy on the move between the cattery and kennel buildings. It was quite apparent that he was in a world of his own, running back and forth from the kennels to the cattery, crisscrossing every which way with his nose low down to the ground sniffing all the new smells that dogs enjoy with his tail wagging high in the air. I could see he was enjoying himself, totally oblivious of me, and couldn't give a 'monkeys' where I was.

You could say I was a little bit annoyed, to be honest, VERY ANNOYED!

Trying to keep the annoyance out of my voice, I called out to Benson as sweetly and softly as possible,

"Benson, Benson. Come to Geoffrey. That's a good boy."

Benson ignored me!

"Come on Benson, that's a good lad."

Benson ignored me!

My temper was rapidly rising, but I didn't want him to sense that I was getting more and more ANNOYED and FRUSTRATED by the second. On hearing my disguised gentle calling, Benson lifted his nose from sniffing what must have been a wonderful scent, looked me straight in the eye and wagged his tail.

'*Got you now, my boy.*'

So, holding the leads that secured the two black Labrador bitches in my left hand, although feeling very angry or even in a severe Benson-killing mood, I did my utmost best to disguise my voice and patted my right thigh.

I called out in the gentlest friendly tone that I struggled to muster,

"Come on Benson, come to Geoffrey. Good boy."

Benson ignored me!

Was he getting to me, or what? I might just as well have been invisible.

I tried again,

"Come on Benson. Good boy."

With my second command that had turned into a plea, he proceeded at high speed, not toward me, but away from me at full steam in the opposite direction and disappeared into our garden. Oh, I can tell you by now I was seething with anger, but I still couldn't let my anger show, or he would have sensed my mood, and I would never have gotten anywhere near the 'Little Sod'.

With my mounting frustration, I could have used a word to describe Benson that was a lot stronger than 'A Little SOD'!

Our garden was fenced in with rabbit netting, as was all the property. So, I had an idea.

'No problem, I'll corner him against the wire.'

But the slippery Benson had other ideas.

He thought it was idyllic fun running around with Geoff and two Labradors chasing after him. He showed no interest in my two gorgeous black beauties, so I stood little or no chance of enticing him back with them.

We have come to the part where I mentioned, take note of Ann's routine.

I was only ten yards away from the cattery where Ann, totally unaware of my situation and rising anger, was feeding the cats. Trying hard to hide my mounting frustration and increasing blood pressure, I shouted rather abruptly,

"ANN! CAN YOU PLEASE COME OUT HERE AND HOLD THESE TWO LABS?"

Note, I did manage to say please!

Ann came out immediately, and after taking one look at my purple glowing face and knowing me so well, she never said a word as she took the two leads attached to the two bemused black beauties. Being free of the Labradors, I was quite confident that this would enable me to catch the flying Benson.

With that, I couldn't wait to set my new plan into action...

Strangling him came to mind!

'Ok, matey. Here comes Geoffrey. Your freedom is coming to an abrupt end.'

With renewed vigour I gave chase. My temper was rising by the second, and I hate to think what my blood pressure was doing. I ran ragged around our cottage clockwise and then anti-clockwise several times whilst imagining what it would feel like to get my hands around his soft furry little throat.

Benson must have read my mind, because ...

He vanished!

Exhausted, I ran to the garden gate and as fit as I was, I flopped on it for support, gasping and gagging for oxygen. As I slowly recovered, I looked up, and the sight that greeted my eyes was way, way, way, beyond my comprehension.

'Jesus Christ, I can't believe what I am seeing.'

Benson was in serious love mode, mounted on top of one of the Labradors that Ann was holding. At the same time, the little Sod was gazing straight at me with his ears pricked up and his tongue lolling. I am sure by the expression on his face, he was saying,

"Hey Geoff, is this good fun or what?"

Ann was completely unaware that he was on top of one of the dogs she was patiently holding. He must have shot behind her so quickly and quietly while she was looking toward the garden for me and, of course, that lunatic Benson.

I screamed out,

"FOR CHRIST'S SAKE ANN. LOOK AT BENSON. STOP HIM!"

She looked down in amazement and finally realised what the sneaky slippery Benson was doing. But by then, so to speak, he was well into the swing of things.

'Jesus Christ!'

The word anger doesn't justify my feelings.

I rushed over to where Ann was standing with her two black companions and the bad boy Benson in full flow. At that moment, I was in a seething temper, and I am afraid I upset Ann with some colourful language. She, in turn, forced the two bitches leads back into my hand and stormed angrily away from my ever-continuing farce back toward the cattery, leaving me with the two black beauties and bad boy Benson. His mischievous eyes were sparkling, and he was still in full love mode, totally ignoring what had transpired between the two angry humans.

I glared at him.

"I'm going to get you now lover boy. If it's the last thing I do!"

As I held the Labrador's leads in my left hand, I made a grab for the slippery fugitive with my right. I completely missed him as he jumped off his placid girlfriend, who didn't seem to have a clue what was going on.

Then the unthinkable happened...

As Ann entered the cattery, the sneaky Benson quickly shot behind and squeezed past her.

I could not believe what my eyes were witnessing.

'OH NO!'

Benson was inside the cattery!

'THE TSUNAMI HAS ARRIVED!'

And that is when the fun really started!

The crazy Benson, let loose in pussycat paradise.

In all of his wildest dreams, he must never have thought that he would get a day like this.

Ann, completely distraught, stood at the cattery door sobbing. As I rapidly slid by her, I stuffed the leads of the two Labradors back into her hand and screamed,

"HOLD THESE LEADS!"

Notice I didn't say please.

I stormed in after the nutter.

I knew he couldn't get to any of the cats because they were all locked away in their separate runs.

But he certainly would be frightening them all, that's for sure.

Benson was running at break-neck speed. He was

almost heeled over on his two right legs as he ran in a clockwise direction around the cream-tiled pathway. The cat runs were on his left side. The startled occupants were hissing, spitting, meowing, flying and ricocheting everywhere. As he passed each cat, he barked at them in his mounting excitement.

From the look on his face, he must have been thinking,

'Is this fun or what?'

The noise in the cattery was increasing—Benson's fun was increasing—Ann's sobbing was increasing—And Geoff's rising blood pressure, frustration and seething temper were increasing.

I bellowed at the top of my voice,

BENSON!

What customers might have thought if they could have heard the racket erupting from the cattery. Benson was yapping, cats were screaming, I was shouting and Ann was sobbing. It was a good job we didn't allow customers on the premises at 6 am!

Benson increased his speed even more; he must have been mesmerised by so many cats yowling with their eyes as big as saucers and ricocheting off the side panels and mesh doors. I joined Benson's new game, 'Ring a ring a roses' in Geoff's prestigious cattery. He was outrunning me and glancing sideways at each cat as he flew by.

And to wind me up, even more, he kept looking back at me with a mischievous grin on his face as if to say,

"It doesn't get any better than this Geoff."

After at least three pandemonium circuits, I reversed direction and made a flying rugger tackle. I caught Benson as he tried to dodge past me and to make my morning even better. Ugh! I experienced a warm wet feeling spreading down my legs as I slid along the once-cream tiles holding the panting Benson next to my body.

The next thing the cheeky devil did was to have the audacity to look into my eyes and lick my face as if to say,

"Hey Geoff, that was great fun. Give us a big

kiss?"

Kiss him; kiss him. I felt like biting him right on the end of his cute shiny black nose. *GRR...NASH!*

I certainly didn't think that episode had been fun at all, especially when I looked down in disgust at my newly-washed jeans. To cap it all, they were covered in brown runny dog excrement, a loving gift from the over-excited Benson.

But how could I be annoyed with such a lovely character?

So, with sheer teeth-gritting determination, I cooled my temper and put him on the lead. Calmly I led him over to the kennels walking very stiffly to keep my disgusting, sticky, smelly, cooling jeans from adhering to my legs. At that memorable moment in time, I must have looked a sorrowful sight.

Through gritted teeth, I said,

"Well young lad you will never, ever be let off your lead again."

He looked up at me, wagging his tail as if to say,

"Hey Geoff, every dog has his day."

To finalise Benson's story, I think it will have been the most exciting day he will ever have in his life. Luckily, the black Labrador bitch could never have become pregnant because she was not in season.

When I returned to the cattery, wearing a second pair of clean jeans, all the cats appeared to be contented as they scoffed their breakfasts as if nothing out of the ordinary had happened. (Typifying the cat breed.) Ann eventually forgave me for shouting at her, and later we laughed together about the eventful fun half-hour we had spent that morning.

Did I say fun?

Kathy had carried on with dog walking, totally oblivious to what had been going on and not wondering where the mischievous Benson and I had disappeared to. And I am sure Benson just felt as if it had been a typical day for him. Benson stayed many more times but was never trusted off his lead. It would have been over my dead body.

No more repeat performances for me, thank you

very much.

Anyway, I suppose one cannot beat a little bit of early morning exercise.

CHAPTER 2

Boisterous Ben

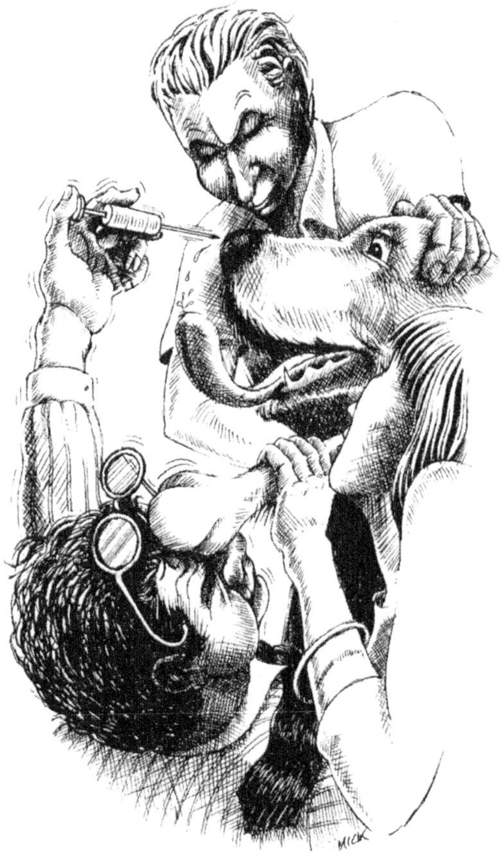

This story is hilarious!

Ben was a cream-coloured Labrador puppy and was only a few weeks old when he first visited us.

Everyone fell in love with him.

It was instant!

Ben's owners, Mr and Mrs Patterson had previously brought Lady, a St Bernard to board with us. Lady is in a future story. She is the gentle giant who put a Doberman named Bruno well and truly in his place as he tried to bully toy dogs. Sadly, Lady had passed away. Fortunately, she was not staying with us at the time.

Ben was her follow-up and was entirely different in all aspects of character and size. He had lovable big, bright brown eyes and looked like the famous 'Andrex' toilet paper advert that was often shown on UK TV. When Ben bounded towards us, his fur and puppy fat rolled from side to side. He grew up into a very handsome, powerful Labrador.

Take note, the powerful part of his character was unfortunate for us.

Or should I say, me!

There is a significant reason for the previous sentences. You will find out very soon.

When Ben had grown to his full size, I think his brain must have been left behind because he always remained a powerful, playful large puppy. Now there's nothing wrong with staying young in the head, even though I still think I am only twenty years old!

But Ben as lovable as he was.

Was totally, un-trainable!

In fact,

HE WAS AN ABSOLUTE HEADBANGER!

If ever you wanted to meet an absolute headbanger, over-friendly Ben, always sporting a mischievous puppy grin on his face was the boy.

Ben came to stay with us most weekends,

probably because his owners had finally realised what an uncontrollable handful he was.

They no doubt thought why not give someone else the task of looking after him so that we can have a well-deserved rest.

It was never my original plan to look after headbangers like Ben. If every dog had been as boisterous and unstoppable as Benny Boy, I don't think I would have lasted five minutes in the running of our boarding kennels side of the business.

I would have been driven mad. A nervous breakdown comes to mind.

We had the pleasure of Ben's company dozens of times over the years and he became a legend in his own time.

Some of the staff adored him, while others did their best to avoid him.

And guess who was right at the very top of that latter list?

ME!

The biggest problem I had walking Ben was trying to get the nutter on his lead as I endured his impatience to get out into the nearby woodland. I must add the rest of the staff had the same problem, but most of them didn't seem to notice or mind. Using his immense strength, he would not stop bouncing about. He almost pushed me over as he planted his large paws on my chest trying to put a wet, slobbery kiss full on my lips. The nutter in his excitement never realised that he was delaying his walk.

When I eventually got the bouncing maniac lassoed with a much-needed choke chain, that was when the fun really started. If you could call it fun! He walked if that is what you would call it, virtually all the way around the woodland dancing on his hind legs totally ignoring the tightening choke chain that made him cough his heart out.

So, what would his front legs be doing?

Well, of course, pawing all over me yet again, covering me with mud or even worse dog crap, because he never cared where or what his feet were landing in.

In my initial attempts to walk Ben, I tried to train him not to jump up, but he was unstoppable. Even a gentle push with my knee in his chest did not affect him at all. He thought everything was a game, and he always seemed to have that same playful grin on his face. I think if I had hit him on the top of his head with a large shovel, it wouldn't have made a blind bit of difference. He would have just grinned at me.

Not that I wanted to hit him on top of his head with a shovel.

A sledgehammer came to mind once or twice!

When it was time for dog walking, on most occasions I craftily made sure that it was someone else who walked Ben. Whoever walked him, (including me) would come back in totally different coloured clothes to the ones they set out. When I say different colour, I mean the peaty colour of woodland mud, especially if it was raining. It seemed to be Ben's main ambition in life to keep washing machines in constant work. Some of the young girls didn't mind because they didn't have to wash their own clothes. Their parents must have wondered what we were doing with their offspring. Maybe we were running mud wrestling classes, not an animal boarding establishment. Well, some of the girls obviously didn't mind getting covered in mud.

But I most certainly did!

By now, you should be getting the picture.

I AVOIDED BEN LIKE THE PLAGUE!

Ben had been coming to us for nigh on four years and was still the same crazy headbanger. Most of that time, I managed to stay well clear of him.

On this occasion, he was staying with us for two boisterous weeks.

When Ben arrived, his owners informed us that they hadn't had time to get him vaccinated against the dreaded kennel cough virus. Kennel cough is a respiratory infection suffered by dogs caused by a wide range of bacteria and viruses. Kennel cough is very bad news for dog boarding establishments. It is highly contagious and goes through the canine guests like a dose of salts. The main symptom is a harsh, hacking cough. Not good when you are chockablock with canine guests. That's for sure!

Fortunately, so far that year, we hadn't been hit by the nasty virus.

Ben's owners asked us whether we could organise the vaccination for them, and they would pay the vet directly. Fortunately, they used the same vet as we did so we knew there wouldn't be any payment problems.

The question is. Did Ben's owners know something we didn't?

OR, MORE TO THE POINT, DID BEN KNOW SOMETHING WE DIDN'T?

These alarming thoughts ran through my head.

'What will Ben's behaviour be towards the vet?'

'Will the vet be able to handle his boisterous superpower?'

This is where I need to mention how the kennel cough vaccination is administered so that you will understand my previous thoughts.

The vaccination isn't an injection as such. Using a syringe with a wide blunt needle, the administrator squirts a chemical liquid deep into the dog's nostrils. And some of our canine friends didn't like it.

IN FACT—THEY DIDN'T LIKE IT ONE LITTLE BIT!

Mind you, I am sure we humans wouldn't like a cold chemical liquid squirted up our nostrils, especially while being restrained.

I can sympathise with the canine tribe because I have had a couple of Covid tests and had an oversized cotton bud violently shoved up my nose by an uncaring nurse. It hurt so much I thought it was coming out of the top of my head, and I couldn't stop sneezing!

So, how was my dear friend Ben going to react to a strange man squirting cold fluid up his nostrils?

That was the million-dollar question.

Well, it wasn't going to be too long before we found out.

Did I say we?

I can assure you, there was absolutely no way, NO WAY AT ALL, I was going to get myself involved in the guaranteed ensuing fracas.

Pat, my manager, is deeply involved in this story.

She is a petite brunette, sporting a pageboy hairstyle, with a ruddy complexion.

I felt sure that the threesome, meaning Pat and one of our young staff Gill, along with the vet, could surely sort Ben out. I stress the point.

WITHOUT ANY HELP FROM ME!

Well, there were three of them. So, what could go wrong?

Anyway, I decided I was going to stay well clear.

The vet was due at 3 pm.

I had a plan...

Shortly after 3 pm, I was leaving the premises.

This is the first part.

I was going to hide in my other office situated in our cottage over a hundred yards away from the forthcoming wrestling bout.

And that is exactly what I did.

The vet Mr Edwards, arrived at 3 pm on the dot.

Good man!

So, hiding behind our mauve velvet curtains and furtively peering through the diamond-leaded window, I watched the vet's blue Volvo Estate pull up outside the kennel office. The vet clambered out of his car and was greeted by Pat and Gill.

Here is the second part of my plan.

The devious part!

I made an excuse to Pat.

I had arranged an appointment with our accountant at 3 30 pm, the same afternoon as the guaranteed wrestling bout.

As I watched Bouncing Ben was led out of the kennel building by Pat. As usual, he was on his hind legs trying to cover his handler in vast amounts of snot and slobber.

The bespectacled vet was standing on the lawn by the carpark waiting to greet the excited

Labrador. Ben spotted the vet as fair game. So, disregarding Pat, he lurched violently toward the vet on his outstretched lead.

BEN WANTED TO FLATTEN HIM!

I wasn't sure who was going to be the patient.

THE VET—OR BEN?

The curtains in our lounge were twitching as I watched with profound amusement the circus-like proceedings with a wry smirk on my face.

Watched by the astonished vet, Ben bounced, twisted, and snorted as Pat tried to control him in his excitement to get to his potential bespectacled friend standing on the grass. After a couple of minutes, Pat helped by Gill just about managed to keel Ben over.

Ben was writhing upside down with all four legs thrashing in the air.

The girls were struggling to hold him.

I was beside myself with amusement.

I laughed out loud.

The vet set about Ben.

Or was it vice versa?

Suddenly, an awful thought crossed my mind.

'OH NO, I've left some papers in the office. I need to get them for the accountant.'

At that moment, the very last thing I wanted in the world was to get myself involved in Ben's melee.

But I am afraid I had no choice, I had to get to the office and walk past the three sporting contestants wrestling on the grass, not forgetting the fun-loving Benny boy.

I feared and knew that it would be an all-in wrestling match with no holds barred.

And there was only going to be one winner!

BEN!

Reluctantly, I plucked up the courage to walk

across the large lawn leading to the office or I would be late for my appointment.

As I attempted to sneak past the three writhing bodies struggling for victory, it looked very much like the human team were losing against the overwhelming power of Ben.

Ben had recovered his position and was on all fours.

Ben was back to full power.

Ben had leverage.

Ben was spinning his attackers round and round on the grass.

Pat landed on her backside with a resounding thud.

Ben was trying to lick her face.

I was only yards from the safety of the office...

To my dismay, Pat spotted me and looked at me with pleading eyes.

As if to say,

'*Any chance of a hand Geoff?*'

I looked back at her with a knowing smile on my face.

'*No way, José. On your bike!*

Pat, on her backside, was desperately hanging on to Ben's kicking back legs. But Ben had regained the advantageous high ground and was in a commanding position.

Gill was struggling with his front legs.

Ben looked as fresh as a daisy.

The vet's glasses had slipped to an acute comical angle.

He tried to get an arm lock around Ben's violently shaking head.

The vet won and Ben went down.

Ben thought it was a new game.

Ben was lying on his back with his mouth open.

Ben had a lopsided grin.

Ben's pale pink tongue was lolling out.

Ben's tail was furiously wagging.

The vet had gone purple in the face.

The vet was sweating profusely.

The vet was struggling to control Ben's head.

The vet was losing.

I smiled to myself as I thought of the high veterinary charges he inflicted on us,

'You're earning your money now mate!'

I went into the sanctuary of my office picked up the necessary papers and was about to walk past the battling foursome.

But...

My conscience kicked in and I just couldn't bring myself to walk away from their desperate situation.

I returned and placed the papers intended for the accountant on my office desk.

The stupid, brave hero, meaning me, walked up to the four heaving bodies, one coated in yellow fur. I volunteered my services. Even though I was dressed in my Sunday best, I could sense there weren't any refusals forthcoming for my offer to help.

I decided to take charge and said,

"As you can see, I'm not dressed for dog wrestling today. So, if I grab hold of Ben's front legs, I should be pretty much, well out of the way."

OR WAS IT—THE FIRING LINE?

"Pat, can you hold Ben's back legs and Gill, can you hold Ben's head for the vet's waiting syringe."

'*What am I doing here?*'

'Am I crazy, or what?'

'How have I got myself involved in this melee?'

Eventually, I got an excellent hold of Ben's flailing front legs.

Pat had hold of Ben's back legs and we managed to turn him over on his back.

Gill was just about managing to hold Ben's head still.

Amazingly, Ben calmed down.

Had Ben run out of steam?

OR WAS THIS THE CALM—BEFORE THE STORM?

Ben had a mischievous glint in his eye.

Did Ben have a plan?

Was I in his plan?

With the extra help coming from me, the vet didn't hesitate and went straight into the attack on Ben's shiny black nostrils.

The vet squirted the vaccine deep inside Ben's nose.

This new sensation had a strange effect on Ben.

A calming effect.

Ben's body went completely limp.

And then...

Benny boy did a bit of squirting of his own.

Ben's aim was deadly accurate!

A powerful jet of golden pee shot straight out of the end of Ben's penis.

Guess where it was aiming?

I saw the golden jet of pee shooting straight at me, as if in a slow-motion movie.

Oh no!

I couldn't get out of the way!

The warm wet jet hit me smack bang in the middle of my forehead then trickled down between my eyes onto my nose.

It felt pleasantly warm.

Not hot, but soothingly warm.

Well, it was a cold afternoon!

The other three contestants never uttered a sound, they just gawped at me in total disbelief.

Immediately, I let go of Ben's front legs and keeping my mouth clenched tightly shut. And I mean very, very tightly shut. I for sure, didn't want to taste or swallow any of Ben's generous golden gift of bodily liquid.

'Jesus! I need a washbasin and quick.'

Luckily, the staff toilet was only fifteen yards away. I ran at full speed with my head bowed well forward in a bid to keep the golden liquid from dripping off the end of my nose into my mouth or onto my new birthday present. A light blue Ralph Lauren shirt. The designer shirt had cost Kathy an arm and a leg. With my body doubled over shaped like the letter L, I raced over to the toilet and had a welcoming wash in the hand basin.

I moved so fast. I was a bit like a 'flash in the pan.' There's a joke there somewhere!

With immense relief, I got to the washbasin with Ben's gift of golden liquid still dripping off the end of my nose and fortunately not on my lips or shirt. I made more than doubly sure that I still had my mouth clenched shut as I set about giving my face the most welcoming wash of its life.

As I tackled the delicate task, I could hear stifled sniggering coming from the car park behind me. I wasn't sure who was sniggering the most. I turned around and looked out the doorway.

It was the vet!

He was wiping tears from his eyes.

I knew it wasn't dog pee in his case.

Pat burst into hysterical laughter as she pointed a finger at me and said,

"Geoff, you have played tricks on me too many times, now this is payback time."

I gave her a look that said, 'What goes around comes around. (Later in this book it does!)

And to cap it all, other staff members came to see what all the fun was about and within seconds, they erupted in laughter.

"HA! HA! HA! HA! HA! HA! HA! HA!"

They just couldn't stop laughing.

And who could blame them?

I must admit, it wasn't long before I saw the funny side of things and I joined in too.

My friend Boisterous Ben just sat there, totally unconcerned, thrashing his powerful tail from side to side.

Ben's big, bright brown eyes were looking directly at me.

AND HE JUST GRINNED AND GRINNED AND GRINNED!

CHAPTER 3

The Dreaded Lurgy

This chapter is more contagious than Covid!

After deadeye Ben's direct hit on my face, this is a necessary VERY SHORT factual chapter about the nasty kennel cough virus. If ever you fancied running a pet boarding establishment or boarding your dog, you should know about this.

By the way, the word lurgy is a slang word which means some kind of disease or ailment. I am sure some of you older readers will remember this. It originates from the nineteen fifties UK radio program, The Goon Show, starring Spike Milligan, Peter Sellers, and Harry Secombe.

Kennel cough is the common name used for canine infectious tracheobronchitis.

My word, that is a mouthful!

Kennel cough is a highly contagious virus which spreads in a similar way to the dreaded disease of foot and mouth. Foot and mouth disease (FMD) is a highly contagious viral disease of animals. It is one of the most serious livestock diseases. It affects cloven-hoofed animals (those with divided hoofs), including cattle, buffalo, camels, sheep, goats, deer, and pigs. Not that we boarded any of those creatures!

August is renowned in the boarding kennel trade for the arrival of the worrying kennel cough virus. I suppose it is Sod's Law that the virus arrives at a boarding kennel when they are at the busiest. To my mind, kennel cough is a crazy name for the virus, because it sounds like it materialises in boarding kennels.

I most certainly know, it does not!

The fact is, the only way the kennel cough virus can arrive at a boarding kennel is by an infected dog. Unfortunately, dog owners never know if their dog has got the infection when they bring it onto the premises. The initial symptoms are not noticeable. An infected dog could have been in residence for three days or more before the staff may have noticed a cough had developed. The virus's major weapon is it is highly contagious well before the infected dog starts coughing.

By that time, it is far, far too late!

Many of the dogs will have caught the airborne virus, and it would already have had a good foothold in the kennels before one could do anything about it. It is a pity that the infected dogs could not talk because they would have been able to let their owners or the kennel proprietor know that they had got a sore throat.

Contradicting the title of this book, in those circumstances we wished they could talk.

We took precautions to ensure that all dogs coming to our establishment were fully vaccinated. We were lucky, we only had the virus a couple of times. As soon as we discovered that the virus had penetrated our front line of defence, meaning vaccinations, we disinfected ourselves in a bid to stop the virus from travelling to the other kennel blocks. We allocated each staff member to work in one block only. We did every possible thing we could to try and stop this irritating nuisance of a virus from spreading.

Sadly, it was usually to no avail.

Unfortunately, like foot and mouth, the virus can travel through the air when a dog coughs or sneezes. If it got windy, and I can guarantee you it always did, the kennel cough was everywhere.

So, the virus won!

Our policy was to cover all the veterinary bills under our insurance. Customers collecting infected dogs would go home with a medication supply, which our vet had already prescribed. We even covered dogs free of the virus for five days after leaving our premises, just in case they developed it later.

Wow, and were there some misunderstanding customers.

And they could be nasty too!

The worst problem was when a dog owner blamed us for infecting their dog. This, of course, could have affected our good reputation. You would not believe how some people responded. They treated us just as if we had spread the virus on purpose.

One angry customer even threatened to sue us because his two dogs had developed a cough a few days after he had collected them. They had puked all over his lounge carpet. I would just like to point out that we did warn our customers before they boarded with us if our premises had acquired the virus, so at least they had the choice to go elsewhere.

In the summer season we had well over one hundred and fifty dogs boarding with us, or even up to our record of two hundred.

Can you imagine what sort of problems could arise?

The virus could even kill older dogs and very young puppies, so we took every possible preventative measure available to us. The massive problem is that there are several different strains of the nasty virus, and one vaccination did not cover all the strains, which is a bit like the flu or Covid vaccination for humans.

If a vaccinated dog contracted the virus, then the cough was not as bad as it could have been without the vaccination.

Unfortunately, the worry of kennel cough was one good reason for me not to look forward to summertime.

Well, that is the factual stuff out of the way.

I am certain you will enjoy the next less serious

chapter about hounds that would give Houdini a run for his money.

RUN, is the operative word!

CHAPTER 4

Houdini Hounds, Dogs On The Run

Sid

When I planned to change my career to a pet boarding proprietor, I most certainly never visualised an event like this first Houdini tale. If I had, it would have horrified me.

This event will get your heart pumping. It certainly did mine!

So, now we come to a mind-blowing frightening adventure of the first Houdini escape artist, and his name is Sid. He is a black mongrel with a strain of Border Collie running through his blood. His owner, Mr James was a very nice gentleman who couldn't praise our facilities enough with all the reports he had heard about our boarding facilities.

After my 'wonderful' Benson experience, I hoped it wasn't for chasing escaping dogs!

Mr James delivered Sid to us without even inspecting our premises. He had been recommended to us by a friend. In my opinion, it was always the best way of expanding our business or anyone else's business. I proudly advised him to have a quick look at our ultra-modern facilities before he left Sid with me. He took me up on my offer and made time for a brief inspection.

After his swift tour, to my great satisfaction, he said,

"I like the look of your premises. I shall have no hesitation in recommending you to everyone I know."

And that was even before Sid had stayed with us. Hearing comments like that from any customer was always an excellent boost to my ego. With that sweet information buzzing in my head, I most certainly had to make doubly sure that he would be more than happy with Sid when he eventually collected him. So there and then I decided I would be the one to take care of Sid personally, just like a VIP, or in Sid's case, a VID (Very Important Dog.)

Mr James advised,

"Sometimes Sid is very clever at slipping his lead."

'Ugh, ugh, here we go again.'

So, to put his mind at rest I answered,

"Don't worry Mr James, I'll personally walk Sid for you twice every day. He looks like my sort of dog, and there's no way he'll slip his lead with me on the other end, I can assure you of that!"

'Famous last words? Or what?'

With a tear in his eye, Mr James handed me the lead with the love of his life safely attached to the other end. He returned to his car, reversed and with his arm out of the window gave Sid a goodbye wave then proceeded down our long drive. Sid was sitting down with his eyes wide open in despair and whining as he intently watched him go.

After Mr James's sad departure, my new VID friend turned and walked with me around the corner of the kennel block and headed across the grass towards the attractive woodland. I looked down at Sid, and he wagged his tail as he looked back up at me with endearing eyes.

I patted his head and said,

"I can see you aren't going to be the slightest bit of trouble at all. Are you Sid?"

He thrashed his tail even more as I bent down and stroked his quivering back. As a precaution, as lovely as he was, I wasn't going to let him get the better of me, so I tightened his collar by an extra notch.

'That should sort you out, my little friend. This is going to be a piece of cake.'

Suddenly, Sid pulled back.

To my horror and utter astonishment, his collar tightened by me only seconds ago slipped right over the top of his head.

My first thoughts were.

'Jesus Christ. How did you do that?'

Sid was free.

He ran like the wind.

He left me standing on the spot, gawping like an

idiot.

De'ja'vu, it was just like watching a movie in slow motion.

Momentarily, I was in complete shock, and my mouth was still agape. I was holding Sid's lead, attached to the empty Sid-less collar, as it slowly swung to and fro.

'OH NO!'

Like grease lightning, Sid headed toward the car park in the direction from whence we had just walked. I quickly got my act together and sprang into action giving chase.

I had to cut him off!

I needed to get past him to get to our five-bar boundary gate before he did. If I made it, I would close it and stop him from making his escape down the drive.

I just had to beat him to that gate!

As I sprinted, I felt I had gone from zero to a hundred miles an hour in less than a second. Believe me, I could run in those days, and I must say, I certainly got plenty of practice. Not forgetting my mate Benson.

I ran like the wind.

'Sid has never been on the premises before. He won't know his way around and hopefully cannot find his way out. Or would he?'

I rounded the corner of the kennel block, but to my dismay, as fast as I had covered the ground, he was fifty yards in front of me and disappearing fast...

Very fast!

He shot around the corner of the silver-birch woodland, which bordered the car park. To my horror, it was looking very much like he was going to die because he was heading straight down the drive in a suicidal dash toward the hazardous highway.

'OH! NO! NO! NO! HE'S GOING TO DIE!'

In sheer desperation, I cut diagonally through the birch wood, trying to head him off and get to the gate before he did. An Olympic hurdler would have had nothing on my turn of speed through that seventy-yard sprint as I hurdled over briars and burst through waist-high bracken.

To my despair…

I was too late!

He had beaten me to the wide-open gate by five dog lengths. Or should I say Sid lengths—the gate that his caring owner had passed through only a minute or so before.

I bellowed,

"SID, SID, COME BACK!"

'No chance!'

Sid was hurtling down the drive like an Exocet missile, desperately chasing after his oblivious owner, who was nowhere in sight.

'Jesus Christ! He is about to get himself flattened on the A41.'

With my heart pumping like a piston engine, I about turned and sprinted off to get my green Daihatsu Jeep. The Jeep was in its usual place parked outside our cottage gate two hundred yards away. I was running so fast I must have scorched the grass. It was usual for me to leave the ignition keys in during the day and often at night. And thankfully today was no exception.

Breathless, I jumped in and slammed the door, thank goodness my old faithful started at the first turn of the key. I knocked the gear stick into reverse and reversed fifty yards flat out with the rear wheels spinning and squealing as they struggled to get traction on the black tarmac. Making that crazy high-speed manoeuvre enabled me to turn around to face our long drive. After that movie stunt of driving, I slammed her into first gear, and away she lurched. It was the fastest three-point turn I had ever made.

And it might just save Sid's life!

I had never driven down our drive so fast. I prayed that no one else was coming up. If anyone was, oh boy, the driver was going to get a very big shock. Especially when a maniac driving a large green blur, representing my Daihatsu Jeep filled their windscreen. It was early morning, and my major worry was that it could have been our speed-loving postman. I had asked him to slow down on many occasions, but he never seemed to listen.

As luck would have it, I didn't kill or even run into the postman or meet any other vehicle. At least something had gone my way.

But could I save Sid's life?

I reached the end of the drive adjoining the A41 and slammed on the brakes. I careered to an emergency stop, with the tyres screeching and smoking.

With my heart pounding away, I looked left and then right. I was distraught!

'Which way has he gone?'

I looked left again, and to my horror, I spotted him. Sid was about two hundred and fifty yards away, just a tiny dot in the distance. He was running flat out along the broken white line in the middle of the road. He was obviously in desperate pursuit of Mr James who was probably halfway home.

'Oh no! Please, No, No, No, Sid! You are going to die for sure!'

Stamping the Jeep's accelerator to the floor

hitting maximum power, I gave chase, and the 4 x 4 careered from the drive entrance, just like Batman's Batmobile rocketing out of his secret cave.

With incredible luck for Sid and for me, it was amazing that there wasn't a car or truck in sight. Believe me, that was an absolute miracle on that dangerous stretch of road. At the speed Sid had shot down our drive, it was a wonder Mr James hadn't seen him in his rear-view mirror. Well, at least I knew there was no way Sid was going to outrun my green rocket. So, with my headlights on and my hazard lights flashing, I sped down the centre of the road with the Jeep's wheels dangerously straddling the broken white line. To complete the picture, all I needed was a siren and a blue flashing light.

Giving the battling-determined Sid a wide berth, I finally overtook him. He appeared oblivious to me transfixed, not unlike a racing greyhound chasing an imitation hare.

After fifty yards, I skidded from seventy miles an hour into a screeching emergency stop. I parked the Jeep with the wheels straddling the central line, a very hazardous manoeuvre indeed. Aghast, I looked up in horror as I saw a massive bright red truck looming in front of me at speed.

High speed!

Momentarily rooting me in my seat.

It looked enormous.

IT WAS ENORMOUS!

Because I was driving with intense concentration, I hadn't noticed the massive truck careering toward me from the opposite direction because I had been too engrossed in watching what Sid the Greyhound copycat was doing in my rear-view mirror. With a loud hissing of air brakes and screaming smoking tyres, the truck driver hit his horn, brakes, and flashers simultaneously. I leapt out of the Jeep, ignoring the massive vehicle as it finally slowed and rolled toward me.

Within a split second, I was around the back of the Jeep and Sid appeared to be tiring. He was only five yards away, trotting towards me, swaying with exhaustion his pink tongue lolling from side to side. It wasn't surprising because he had run flat-out for almost a mile.

He jinked!

I side-stepped!

He jinked!

I side-stepped!

In desperation, he tried to dodge past me.

I was having none of it.

I towered in front of him and screamed at the top of my voice,

"SIT DOWN... NOWWWWWWW!"

Sid was so shocked by the force of my screaming Sergeant Major's voice, his backside immediately hit the tarmac, sitting him down so fast it was a wonder he didn't burn it.

'I always knew I was a good dog trainer!'

Before Sid had time to bat an eyelid, I lunged forward and grabbed him with my right hand by the scruff of his neck. In one swift movement, I lifted him clean off his feet and with my other hand opened the back door of the Jeep and catapulted him safely inside slamming the door behind him.

'Wow!'

With my heart still thumping, I looked behind in the direction from whence we had raced. To my amazement, there were a dozen or so cars parked up with their hazard lights flashing as the occupants keenly watched our exciting death-defying entertainment. With so much preoccupation, I had been oblivious to any other vehicles on the road. I waved a quick, gratifying thank-you to the line of cars and jumped back into the Jeep. Not forgetting to wave another big thank-you to my truck-driver friend sitting high up in his red cab, which was parked with the yellow hazard lights flashing only a few feet in front of my Jeep. Also, I could see a long stream of traffic behind his truck, patiently waiting for his self-made roadblock to clear.

That heart-stopping event, which took place in the middle of the busy main highway, had taken no more than twenty seconds in duration. I can assure you it felt more like a lifetime. It is a heart-thumping memory I will never forget. Sid was stowed safely in the back of the Jeep, and thankfully no accidents had occurred. Fortunately, I was still in one piece as well. Sid had no idea how incredibly lucky he, or should I say, WE, had been.

After that more than exciting escapade, I nicknamed him, 'Sid the Slip'.

Do you know? He never slipped his lead again. Now, why do you think that was? Because I put a choke chain on him every time I walked him. So that cured an almost tragic problem. I am sure you can guess what went on his card outside his run in sizeable red writing:

WARNING SID MUST ALWAYS BE WALKED ON A CHOKE CHAIN. THIS BOY CAN SLIP HIS COLLAR.

I would sooner have taken the slight risk of strangling the little devil with a choke chain rather than see him flattened by an enormous truck. Sid came to us many times after his and my first traumatic experience. I never told his contented owner about Sid's suicidal adventure. Well, would you? And as far as I am aware, Sid didn't tell his dad either.

Yet another cattery & kennel secret bites the dust.

Sid was the first dog, but unfortunately not the last one to escape outside our boundary through that five-bar gate, as you will find out later in this chapter.

But first, we come to a frightening story about Ann, Kathy's sister.

Samson

It was around 6 pm on a cold November night. Ann was outside feeding the cats in the cattery building, and Kathy was preparing our evening meal. I sat relaxing in the lounge in front of an open log fire with my feet up. I was watching the latest news on BBC TV. The curtains were closed making the cottage feel warm and cosy. As I took in the latest information from the glamorous female newsreader, the smells drifting from the kitchen were tantalizing my taste buds, making my ravenous tummy rumble.

Suddenly, Kathy came bursting into the lounge, ruining my repose,

"GEOFF. QUICK! Turn the telly down. I can hear weird noises outside."

I grabbed the remote and pressed mute, instantly killing the sound. We listened, and then to our concern, there was a terrible noise outside...

It sounded very much like a woman screaming.

It was a woman screaming!

Kathy's eyes opened wide with horror.

She shouted,

"OH NO! ANN IS STILL OUTSIDE!"

Following Kathy's concerned sisterly outburst, I immediately shot out of my armchair, ran into the hallway and grabbed the front door knob. I whipped the door wide open, not knowing what I was going to find on the other side. As I looked along the porch-lit pathway and over the garden gate I could see Ann's little red Ford Fiesta parked by my green Daihatsu. The strange thing was, the Daihatsu's interior light was on, and I found it extremely odd to see Ann sitting in the passenger seat, looking directly away from me.

I ran down the path, grabbed hold of the driver's door and attempted to wrench it open, but to my surprise, it was locked. I banged on the window. As Ann turned toward me, she screamed and recoiled, her shocked eyes were wide open. Thankfully, relief flooded over her face as she recognised me, but sadly she had tears mixed with black mascara streaming down her face. I rushed to the passenger door to find out what was going on.

I wrenched the door open and began firing a stream of questions at Ann who appeared to be very distraught,

"Why are you sitting in here?"

"What's wrong?"

"What happened?"

"Why are you crying?"

The questions were rolling off my tongue so quickly that I didn't even give her time to answer.

Ann was very close to being hysterical and through her sobbing spluttered,

"I've been attacked!"

"WHAT?"

'I was thinking in terms of a sex maniac.'

"I'll kill him!"

"Where's he gone?"

"Has he hurt you?"

Through her sobs, she managed to stutter in a shaky voice,

"No, it wasn't a man. It was an animal!"

"What do you mean, an animal?"

"Are you ok?"

"Yes, I am now."

"What kind of animal was it?"

She sobbed even more and said,

"It was a giant dog, big, hairy and heavy. It came from behind, jumped on my shoulders and nearly knocked me over."

Although Ann is only five feet two inches tall, I realised the dog, whatever breed it was, must have been pretty big to have reached her shoulders.

She spluttered more words through her sobbing,

"When I screamed, it ran off. I ran to your vehicle because it was the closest thing to me. Thank goodness you hadn't locked the passenger door. I have been screaming and blowing the horn for ages. Why didn't you come out earlier?"

"I am sorry, but I had the TV on, and Kathy was in the kitchen. I didn't hear you until she came running in to say she could hear strange noises outside."

Eventually, with gentle, soothing words, I managed to comfort and persuade Ann to get out of the vehicle and go to the safety of the welcoming, warm cottage.

I said,

"Ann, please don't worry. I'll get you a nice big brandy to calm your nerves."

I knew that would persuade her. With a brief smile, her eyes lit up in anticipation of my offer. Once she was safely inside the cottage with a glass of amber liquid in her hand, I could see she was a little calmer after her stressful ordeal.

I informed the worried sisters,

“I’m going outside to find out what is going on around here.”

My suggestion alarmed Kathy and she said,

“Aren’t you taking your gun with you?”

Although I am a staunch conservationist, I owned a double-barrelled 12-gauge shotgun. I had retained it from my previous days as a gamekeeper to use in clay pigeon shooting competitions.

Not dog shooting!

I said,

“Surely, you’re not serious?”

“Of course, I’m serious. You don’t know what's out there. "

"Do you?”

Ann piped up,

“I’m not kidding you, Geoff. Whatever kind of dog it was, it was enormous.”

I could tell Ann was still in severe shock by her language.

Kathy, in her wisdom, still thought I needed some form of protection and said,

"Well, at least take a stick with you, especially if that animal is as big as Ann says it is."

To put both their minds at rest, and I must admit mine, I decided to take one of my hazel walking sticks with me, the type that has a 'V' at the top. Also, I grabbed my rechargeable torch that was as powerful as car headlights. I often used it to scan the grounds to check that everywhere was secure.

So, off I went on my exciting adventure with, I must say, just a little bit of trepidation, ensuring that I was careful enough to hide my cautious feelings from the concerned sisters. With exaggerated bravado, I went out into the oily blackness of the cold winter's night and flashed the powerful beam scanning our enclosed ornamental grounds. But I saw nothing and heard nothing. Even though it was as quiet as the grave, I decided to check the inside of the kennel block through the office window rather

than entering the kennel block and disturbing our
slumbering guests.

Arriving outside the office door, I noiselessly unlocked it and crept across the carpet to look through the window from where I was able to observe the deathly quiet kennel block. For a few minutes, I carefully studied each run. I didn't want to turn any lights on because it would have disturbed our guest's canine dreams, and that would have been the end of a peaceful night for every occupant.

As my eyes adjusted to the darkness, I could see that all the gates to the runs were closed. I couldn't see any dogs in their runs at all, probably because it was a cold night and they would be sleeping or resting in their cosy heated quarters.

'Well, if it's a big dog that has escaped, then at least it isn't from our kennels.'

Feeling a little bit puzzled, I left the office and started to make my way back to the cottage. As I did so, a vixen (female fox) eerily screamed out, a sound that never fails to send shivers down my spine. It is a virtual guarantee to hear that same shrill scream in virtually every horror movie.

'All I need now is an owl to hoot, and that will really set the scene.'

Anyway, I was quite determined nothing, but nothing was going to frighten me. I turned the flashlight on again and scanned the grounds all around me. Nothing stirred. Well, that was it. There is nothing out here, so whatever kind of dog it was, it must have gone.

Slightly disappointed that I hadn't solved Ann's mystery, I headed directly back to our cottage to get my much-needed dinner. I was absolutely starving, and my stomach started to rumble again in anticipation. With all the excitement, I had forgotten just how hungry I was. As I was passing through the garden gateway, I heard heavy panting right behind me...

'What is that?'

To my horror, I half-turned around as something big and furry came into view and hit me with considerable force right between my shoulder blades.

I yelled out in alarm,

"JESUS CHRIST!"

I spun around with my stick at the ready, and at that moment, I wished I had my gun because my heart rate had gone right off the Richter scale. To my surprise, standing in front of me was a monstrous long-haired German Shepherd dog. To my relief, it was wagging its tail.

Using a soft voice I patted my right thigh and said,

"Come here. Good dog."

With no hesitation, the large dog bounded straight at me with its tail thrashing from side to side. In its excitement, it launched its two front paws onto my chest, resulting in me breathing in hot doggy breath. It was doing its utmost best to lick my face. I could see it had a collar on, so I quickly grabbed hold of it and pulled the dog off me back onto all fours, all it wanted to do was play with me, not eat me. I must say, it was rather boisterous. No wonder it had frightened poor old Ann out of her wits.

I said,

"Hey, boy. Where the devil, have you come from?

I don't recognise you as being one of ours."

I hung onto the big boy's collar with difficulty because the giant German Shepherd must have thought we were playing some sort of game as it playfully bounced all over the place. With my fingers wrapped tightly under its collar, I managed to drag him to the side of the cottage, where I banged on the study window to alert Kathy.

I shouted,

"KATHY. QUICK, GET ME A DOG LEAD AND TELL ANN I'VE GOT SOMETHING TO SHOW HER."

With that, Kathy passed me a lead through the window, which I managed to secure to the excited more than friendly stranger's collar.

I said to Kathy,

"I've never seen this dog before. It's not from here."

"Oh, yes, he is. He came in today just before we closed. His name is Samson."

Ann arrived at the front door. I laughed

mischievously and said,

“Hey Ann, let me introduce you to cuddly Samson, your little attacker. He’s as friendly as they come.”

Ann retaliated,

“It’s not funny, Geoff. He really frightened me.”

Ann didn’t see the funny side of things, but I was sure she would do very soon.

‘I’ll give her another brandy after dinner that will calm her down.’

After my jesting, I felt sorry for Ann and said,

“I can understand why he frightened you. He did the same to me.”

Anyway, back to the serious stuff. Or was the former serious?

We had no idea how Samson could have possibly gotten out. We knew the only way out of his kennel was through the gate of his run and then he would have had to get out through the main security door of the kennel block. Forgetting my rumbling stomach, I was more than curious and was determined to solve the Samson mystery as soon as possible.

I said,

"Kathy. Where in the kennel block is he from?"

"He was down the right-hand side in the very end kennel."

"Ok, I'll take him back and find out how on earth he managed to get out."

A playful Samson and I walked back down to the kennels to install him again. Hopefully for good this time. Unfortunately, I had to switch on the kennel block lights, which immediately disturbed the sleeping dogs and made them erupt into an excited barking frenzy. I for sure knew that it was going to get much worse when Samson and I walked in. I also knew that most of them would be thinking they were going out for an extra evening walk or maybe getting a nice tasty night-time snack.

I shouted,

"HEY, YOU LOT BE QUIET!"

Gradually, they stopped barking as Samson and I walked down the aisle with the curious canine guests staring at us from either side. Fortunately, most of them quietened down after my loud Sergeant Major's command. Appreciating the silence, I walked the Houdini Hound to his run at the far end of the kennel block. His run bordered the oak woodland where we walked the dogs. I was puzzled, because his gate was securely locked, so that couldn't have been his escape route.

'So how on earth has the big lad got out'?

As I opened the gate to the run and led him in, I looked around at ground level and noticed nothing untoward. I stared up at the corrugated translucent fibreglass roof on the woodland side. I knew there was a small gap between the mesh and the top because it was me who had assembled the steel framework and fixed the corrugated fibreglass roof above. The opening was no more than twelve inches deep and over six feet high from the run's concrete floor. I would never have dreamed that a big dog like Samson or any other dog could scale a six-foot-high barrier, let alone squeeze through such a small gap. But Samson, the little devil, had achieved that incredible feat.

Did I say little? He was enormous!

I locked Samson in his sleeping quarters for the night because I needed to fill in the gap the following day. If I had left him with access to his run, I hate to think where he might have ended up.

Or, who else he would frighten to death?

The first thing next morning, my new mate Samson supervised as I used some wire mesh from a roll leftover from when I originally built the kennels. With the aid of a step ladder, it only took me thirty minutes to complete the job of filling in the troublesome gap. Therefore, my enormous furry mate was not inconvenienced for too long. I hoped he had enjoyed his night out on the tiles because I was sure it was going to be his last. Well, on our premises anyway. And, I am certain Ann would reiterate those last few words.

So, that is how I met my mate Samson, the harmless Houdini Hound.

Now it is the turn of another Houdini Hound, the

incredibly agile Ozzie.

Ozzie

Over the years, we had a large variety of dogs boarding with us, and you would be amazed just how many of them were able to scramble and attain a height of six feet. The number of times we saw dogs climbing the high sides of the steel mesh was unbelievable. They could even give a squirrel a run for its money. The most agile dog was Ozzie, named because his owners loved visiting Australia. With a name like that, you would think he was an Australian outback hound of some sort, but no, he was a beautiful three-year-old black and white Welsh Border Collie with a mischievous glint in his eye. A squirrel in drag!

Ozzie's first stay with us was a six-week stint. Guess where his owners vacationed?

Australia, of course!

Ozzie's owners, Mr and Mrs Phelps, stepped into my office. I went through the compulsory routine of checking his vaccination certificate. Everything was in order, so we went outside onto the car park and retrieved a very excitable Ozzie from the back of their car, a white Nissan hatchback. Immediately, I took to young Ozzie and decided I would take care of him personally, especially as he was boarding with us for such a lengthy stay. Ozzie never gave his owners a second glance as I took him on the standard introductory woodland walk. After the walk, which we both enjoyed immensely, I put him in run number five and then went to get him one of our stainless-steel water bowls.

When I came back holding the filled bowl, to my disbelief, he wasn't there.

WHAT?

I just could not believe my eyes.

I scratched my head in puzzlement. Slowly, I walked down the right-hand row of runs scrutinizing each one. Eventually, and to my absolute amazement, there was Ozzie in kennel number nine.

Had I put him in the wrong kennel?

For sure, I was too young to be losing my memory.

Was I going mad, or what?

Thinking that maybe I was going prematurely senile, I put him back in his original run, number five and never thought any more of it.

Later that day, one of the girls went into the kennel block to find young Ozzie with an apparent big grin on his face sitting proudly in the end run, number twelve. If you remember, this used to be Samson's kennel. Well, at least it was well-proven that I hadn't lost my mind.

On numerous occasions during that first day, we took Ozzie back to the correct run, but as soon as we had turned our backs, he hurdled right back to the other end. After each astonishing performance, he was proudly standing in a new run alongside a friendly, curious occupant. He looked to have been working very hard as he stood panting. He must have thought he was playing a game; well, for sure, he was undoubtedly playing my patience. This dog could be a member of the squirrel family. Fortunately, we had no aggressive dogs boarding with us at that time because if we had, it could have been disastrous for poor Ozzie. Fortunately, he couldn't escape out of the block because the end run had been secured by me previously during the Samson scenario.

Ozzie's feats were incredible; he made Olympic hurdlers look like beginners. And Ozzie's hurdles were over six feet high. A member of the S.A.S. would never have been able to get over the barriers half as fast as our Ozzie. All these crazy thoughts reminded me from a few years back of the British Olympic hurdling hero Colin Jackson, he and Ozzie had something in common besides hurdling. They were both Welsh!

Young Ozzie created a lot of work for me because the gap I had filled in at the top of Samson's run was duplicated all the way down the kennel block on both sides resulting in me buying some more steel mesh. I measured how much material I would need for one gap and then multiplied it by twenty-two which was the total of runs. I completed the work in two days. On reflection, Ozzie had done me a big favour because if he could hurdle from one kennel to another, sooner or later, other agile guests would do the same and no doubt eventually run into...

BIG, BIG TROUBLE!

TROUBLE could have materialised in the form of a large bad-tempered guest, who wouldn't have been too happy in sharing his or her run with an uninvited visitor. There could have been blood and dog bits everywhere, or should I say murder at the kennels. I hate to think what could have happened. How do you explain to an owner returning from a relaxing holiday that all the stitches holding their poor dog together was because it could climb into another dog's territory?

I couldn't say,

"Well, it was your dog's fault he went on a hurdling expedition to visit Big Bruno in the far kennel."

Well, would they believe me? Somehow, I don't think so.

Sadie

This next little Houdini hound caused me two sleepless nights.

All the fun of running a boarding kennel!

Sadie was a black and white female Cocker Spaniel. A Cocker Spaniel is a bit like an English Springer Spaniel but much smaller. SMALL is the keyword for this short story. After Ozzie did me that great favour of pointing out the twenty-two gaps separating each run, I thought all the escape routes were sealed off and escape from our kennels was nigh-on impossible.

However, I was shortly about to find out just how wrong one can be!

Sadie, belonged to a likeable middle-aged couple, Mr & Mrs Timmis. Sadie had been an exemplary guest of ours in August the year before and had been no trouble at all, so eagerly we looked forward to having her back.

Little did I know how different things were going

to be with her second visit.

If I had known what that little dog would do with my stress level, I would most certainly have thought twice about boarding her again.

After thirteen (unlucky for some) days in Sadie's two-week stay, disaster finally struck.

And I mean disaster, with a capital D.

Within five minutes of the staff starting their working day at the usual time of 8 am, Pat phoned me using the office line connecting to our cottage.

Sounding unusually distressed, she said,

"Geoff. Sadie, the little Cocker Spaniel, has gone."

Puzzled, I asked,

"What do you mean gone?"

"Gone ... as in disappeared ... vanished ... not there anymore!"

'Well, it couldn't be much more precise than that.'

Do you ever feel that you have had a conversation like this before, and somehow you know you will have a bad day?

A very, very bad day!

I sprinted across the lawn to the kennels as if I was about to break a world record. In trepidation, I opened the outside security door, stepped inside, and ran down to the kennel run where I knew Sadie should be. I looked inside, and there was Pat blotchy-faced with tears in her eyes.

She sobbed,

"I'm so, so, sorry, Geoff."

Pat was distraught, so trying to console her, I said,

"Don't worry. It most certainly isn't your fault. I'm the one who designed and built these so-called escape-proof kennels."

I checked Sadie's sleeping quarters and all the others in that block. Alas, it was true. The little devil had vanished right off the face of the planet. Pat and I were in absolute shock. The mystery was, how on earth had she escaped?

And the sixty-four-thousand-dollar question was...

Where is she now?

I could not understand why she wanted to escape. She had been quite happy staying with us during the previous twelve days. The bad news was, she was due to be collected in the next two days.

'You naughty, naughty, little dog!'

I can assure you that you do not want to know what dark thoughts I was really thinking.

I entered Sadie's vacant run and got down on my hands and knees. I examined the bottom of the galvanised frame at the front of the run and gate. I scrutinised every bit of the framework and noticed some tufts of loose hair. I picked them up holding them between my thumb and forefinger. To my dismay, I realised that the hair matched Sadie's coat. It wouldn't have taken much of a detective to conclude that Sadie had managed to squeeze under the framework. I found it unbelievable that this was her pathway to freedom because there was only a four-inch gap between the steel frame and the concrete. For some unknown reason, that I will never know, there was a slightly larger gap under the steel framework in this run than the other runs. So, after Sadie's miraculous escape, we ensured that no dogs as small as Cocker Spaniels were ever boarded in that block of kennels again. In the newer kennel blocks, there was only a one inch gap under the steel framework, so that is where all the small dogs were boarded.

I concluded that once out of her run, Sadie must have made her way to the compound gate leading to the woodland path. I hurried over to it, and for the second time in five minutes, I got down on my hands and knees where there was a small drainage gully. I examined the bottom of the steel frame by running my hand underneath it. I stared at the contents in my palm.

'Oh no! More hair! It matches Sadie's.'

I roared in sheer frustration,

"ARRRGH!"

I called out for Jenny, one of my staff, who was scouting around the grounds looking for Sadie,

"JEN QUICK, run as fast as you can down the drive and shut the five-bar gate. She might still be inside our grounds."

I hoped that Sadie hadn't gone through the boundary gate in the short time since the girls had arrived for work. The grounds were fully secured once the gate was closed because we had a wire mesh fence around the perimeter serving two purposes. The first one was to keep any loose dogs in, and the second was to keep the large population of rabbits out. I had erected the five-feet-high fence myself. I sincerely hoped the little Cocker wouldn't have had the initiative and the ability to scramble over it. Unfortunately, rabbits occasionally found a way of burrowing under the netting, even though it was buried and turned outward at the bottom. I hoped Sadie didn't think like a rabbit.

After Jenny had closed the gate, I checked every square inch of the perimeter fence, and there appeared to be no rabbit tunnels or attempted scrapings anywhere. And more to the point, no hole made by Sadie. All the staff diligently searched inside and outside our grounds, but to no avail. I had a horrible 'Déjà Vu Sid feeling that I had been down this road before.

I ran down the driveway to the boundary gate

and checked the wire mesh netting, which had been securely attached by me using a hammer and staples. I had even stapled a stiff black plastic skirt to the bottom of the gate to stop rabbits from squeezing underneath. I thought, with all my security, it was getting like Fort Knox.

I checked the gate where it closed against a sturdy oak post. I bent down and noticed a gap of about four inches between the gate and the base of the post.

'Surely she could not squeeze through there.'

But she had!

Because I found more dog hair matching Sadie's.

No doubt about it!

'OH! NO! NO! NO!'

Now I knew for sure. Sadie was no longer on our grounds.

She had escaped!

For sure, the boundary gate had been her escape

route. Sadie was small but very strong for her size. During the night or early morning, she had pushed and squeezed through gaps just like a mole in its tunnel, making a mockery of my Fort Knox security.

'OH NO!'

I knew that if I didn't act quickly, it would be a dead cert that little Sadie was going to be a dead dog, squashed, and flattened on the busy A41 highway that was waiting for her at the bottom of our drive.

I ran full-tilt for my Daihatsu Jeep. It was parked in its usual spot in front of our cottage gate about two hundred and fifty yards away. All this running kept me tremendously fit, but don't ask what the stress factor was doing to me. Gasping for breath, I jumped into the Jeep, fortunately she started immediately. I realised I had to be very careful not to speed too fast down the drive because maybe a miracle would materialise in the form of Sadie coming back up to our welcoming arms.

'Am I clutching at straws here, or what?'

I thought there might be a very slight chance,

and I mean a very slight chance, that Sadie could have been coming back after her night out on the tiles because, by that time, she should have been quite hungry. The last thing I wanted was to run her over. Now wouldn't that have been something? The proprietor killing a customer's dog.

I drove very carefully down the drive and saw no sign of Sadie. I parked at the bottom where it joined the busy A41 highway and climbed out of the Daihatsu. I was holding some tasty dog treats in my hand as I searched the area calling in a soft, friendly tone,

"Sadie, Sadie. Come here, good girl."

Sadly, there was no sign of her. In utter despair, I jumped back into the Daihatsu and slowly drove down the busy main road for two miles in one direction and then U-turned and travelled in a similar distance in the opposite direction. But nothing, absolutely nothing. There was not a flattened Cocker Spaniel in sight. At least that made me feel a little bit better and that was the good news on that dreadful morning. Reluctantly, I drove back to our cottage and phoned the police, hoping that someone might have handed her over or reported her running along the road. And guess what?

Nothing!

What on earth could I do? Nothing, absolutely nothing, but wait to hear from the police. Hopefully, some kind soul would save Sadie's life and take her to the nearest police station and, with my rising stress level, save my life as well. Countless times that traumatic day I went down to the end of the drive to call and search for Sadie. The day progressed sadly into night, and there was no news.

Good or bad!

When I woke up the next morning, I felt drained of no sleep with the worry and the more than likely death of Sadie. Also, the concern of having to break the sad news to her owners. Just before I was about to leave the cottage and renew my search, the phone rang, jolting me out of my gloomy thoughts. It was Mr Hendry, one of the three partners from the veterinary practice that we used.

He said,

"Have you lost a dog?"

'Have we lost a dog? Have we lost a dog? You bet we have. And I've lost a good night's sleep as well.'

I replied calmly with the hope of an ensuing miracle whilst hiding my fears and frustration,

"Yes, I am afraid we lost one yesterday, a Cocker Spaniel. I have searched high and low. I have also notified the police. Unfortunately, they have heard nothing."

"Well, Geoff, I have a bit of news for you. About twenty minutes ago, I was driving along the A41 when I saw a Cocker Spaniel trotting along the grass verge near the end of your drive. I stopped my car, and as I got out, it ran off into the woodland on your side of the road."

I thanked him for his trouble, slammed down the phone and in excited anticipation, rushed off to my waiting vehicle to do a repeat performance of the day before. Well, at least she was alive. But I was sure it wouldn't be for much longer if she tried to cross that very busy road with the usual multitude of murderous trucks thundering along it.

Parking at the bottom of the drive, I searched for minutes that rapidly turned into hours. Yet again

—nothing, nothing at all.

So, where on earth was she hiding? Didn't she realise what she was doing to my shattered nerves? Anyway, after three hours of heart-stopping searching, I reluctantly returned to the kennels with my 'tail between my legs'. A very appropriate saying for the way I felt at that moment. During that day, we had four more phone calls from various people reporting that they had seen a Cocker Spaniel on the verge of the main road by the end of our drive.

Well, where else would she be?

'Why is everybody else seeing this dog and not me?'

After each phone call, I rushed down the drive to search for her. But no Sadie. Each time I stayed a little longer, waiting for her to come out of her hiding place. I felt sure she was nearby and, to add to my frustration, probably watching every move I made. I called out her name repeatedly and waited for hours, sitting and watching from my vehicle. But, still, no Sadie. It was looking very much like I would have to face another night of worry and no sleep.

'Marvellous! I thought this was going to be a new

career with no stress. And they're meant to be collecting the little devil tomorrow.'

On the dreaded morning of Sadie's collection, I woke up from a very disturbed sleep with the realization that little Sadie would not be there to welcome her owners. I was dreading the moment of telling them the bad news. I mean, everybody's dog is virtually a member of their family, and Sadie was wandering around the woodland or up and down the highway as free as a bird. Imagine coming back off a beautiful tranquil holiday, having relieved yourself of all the stress you accumulated throughout your working year and being told that some idiot boarding proprietor had lost your lovely dog.

Not surprisingly, I had sarcastic thoughts,

'Oh, I'm so sorry, but I've lost your little dog, she has run off into the woods and we can't catch her. But the good news is, she was spotted several times yesterday playing amongst the trucks on the main highway.'

Surely life can be better than this. Only a miracle could save her now.

And here comes the miracle...

At precisely eight-fifteen on the morning of Sadie's collection, a miracle did happen, for who should pull onto our carpark but our vet Mr Hendry.

And guess what?

When he got out of his vehicle, the elusive Sadie walking by his side, thankfully secured on a lead. I could have kissed Sadie and even the vet as well. Frankly, Sadie was a lot better looking than the vet. At least she did have the advantage of being female. And she did not sport a beard either!

Anyway, less of my frivolity, I could not thank him enough. Sadie looked incredibly fit and didn't appear to have lost any weight at all. Her black and white coat was shining, and as a bonus, her stumpy tail was wagging like crazy.

It crossed my mind,

'How many rabbits have you eaten to be in that superb condition?'

Sadie's owners came to collect her later that day, and I couldn't wait to tell them all about their little dog's adventures in the woods. Am I flipping kidding or what?

The excited couple had no idea what had happened to Sadie over the last three days, and as far as I was concerned, that was the way it was going to stay. A smiling Pat brought Sadie out of the kennels to be greeted by her owners, and they thought she looked terrific.

Mrs Timmis, with a sparkle in her eye, said,

“Oh, she looks so happy. She’s even put on some weight as well.”

‘Must have been all the rabbits she has eaten.’

I looked happy as well, but it was no surprise that I had lost weight. I wonder why? And Mrs Timmis never even noticed!

Pat and I gave each other a knowing look as we informed Sadie’s delighted owners how good she had been and how she had been no trouble at all. We emphasised how much we could not wait to have her back again. Were we joking, or what?

Well, at least that little story ended up with a happy ending resulting in smiles all around.

The stark fact was, it was a lot easier for dogs to escape from our clutches than cats, quite simply because we exercised the dogs around the woodland.

We didn't exercise cats!

And yes, we did have some escape artists just like my mate Benson. But fortunately, after a lot of excitement, trauma, frustration and effort, we eventually got them back. Sadie was the last dog to make a complete escape. A few dogs tried, but they never made it because by then, I had plenty of unplanned training and got to that five-bar gate before they did.

If you think that story was traumatic, check out this next painful cat experience inflicted on yours truly.

CHAPTER 5

A Very Painful Conversation

At the start of my exciting new career, I worked alone. Therefore, answering the phone was a problem. We had an answering machine, but I didn't trust potential customers to leave a message.

In those far-off days, not only did many people dislike the idea of using a new-fangled answering device, it occurred to me that they might have thought we weren't even on the premises, therefore the animals in our care would have been left unattended. Furthermore, when customers did leave a message, it was often quite garbled and difficult to decipher. This ongoing problem made me decide to purchase a mobile phone.

At that time, mobiles were a lot larger and far more cumbersome than today's modern state-of-the-art smartphones. So, after a lot of deliberation, I chose a cream-coloured Swiss-made telephone with two handsets. The radio base was in the office and was a bit like a walkie-talkie. I carried the other large handset in a pocket of my shirt, where it fitted quite snugly. If I didn't have a shirt pocket, I held it in my hand because no way would it fit into the tight pocket of my jeans. After all, it was just too big.

We had a lady customer whose name was Mrs Jones. She owned a beautiful Siamese cat named Silky, she used to come and stay with us regularly. We got to know each other very well, and being very affectionate toward me, she loved to be picked up and cuddled. In fact, she always insisted on it. Of course, I do mean the cat and not Mrs Jones.

As previously arranged, Mrs Jones turned up with Silky in her carrier. After checking Silky's vaccination certificate records, Mrs Jones handed the carrier to me containing the love of her life. Immediately Silky looked up at me and pressed her head against the white plastic-coated mesh. That was the nearest she could get to my hand and she was mewing quite loud, as Siamese tend to do.

Mrs Jones said,

"The way Silky is performing, it is quite obvious that she can't wait to get to you."

The good lady didn't realise just how accurate her words were going to be!

Mrs Jones usually came down with me to the cattery to ensure that Silky was installed contentedly. But this time, because Silky had stayed with us so many times, she decided to trust me to do it.

Little did I know, it was about to turn out to be a big, big problem that I will never forget!

So, after saying goodbye to Silky and me, Mrs Jones boarded her car and set off down the drive leaving me to carry the Siamese down to the cattery. As I was carrying the cat carrier, Silky was purring and mewing non-stop. Holding the carrier with my left hand and her soft sleeping bed with my right, I went in through the cattery's outer steel-mesh security door. Then I walked along the left row of cat runs and stopped in front of one that I had prepared that morning.

Stepping inside, I closed the mesh door of her temporary home and locked it with the sliding bolt. I looked down at Silky in her carrier. She was still purring loudly. As I looked at her, she pushed her head even harder against the top of the carrier, obviously begging for me to let her out. I could see she was getting quite impatient at being cooped up for so long.

Very impatient indeed!

I said softly,

"Hang on, darling. I won't be a sec."

I bent down, slid the fastener of the carrier, and flipped it open. With that, Silky jumped straight out.

And that is when the fun started...

For Silky, but certainly not for me!

Ignoring Silky, I started to arrange her soft bedding inside the cream melamine sleeping box on the shelf that was about waist high. As I did so, she pressed and rubbed her body against my calves, purring and mewing loudly. At that precise moment, the handset in my shirt pocket started to ring. I could see it had startled Silky slightly, but I had to answer it. I retrieved it from my shirt pocket and held it in my left hand. On the end of the line was a potential customer, a lady who wanted to inspect the cattery before making her first booking. We always encouraged inspections because we were proud of our premises, and virtually everyone who saw our facilities was impressed. From experience, we knew they would inform their friends and recommend us, sometimes even before their pet had stayed at our establishment.

Remember Sid's dad?

I was thoroughly engrossed in full sales mode with my potential customer. In the meantime, Silky had jumped onto the shelf where there was space in front of the sleeping box. I watched her as she looked at me lovingly. But she just couldn't understand why I was ignoring her.

Her mewing and purring became louder and louder, almost as if she was asking,

"Why haven't you picked me up for my usual cuddle?"

I mentioned to the lady on the phone that I was actually in the cattery installing a regular guest. At that precise moment, Silky lost her patience and decided she wanted her usual cuddle.

NOW!

Right now, and I mean now!

With that, she launched herself off the shelf, straight at me, with her razor-sharp claws extended.

She flew like a guided missile and landed on my chest.

Just as if I was a tree.

But I wasn't a tree.

I was a delicate human being.

Silky's front feet landed on my chest and her back feet on my stomach. She was so close to my face; her dainty nose was virtually touching my not-so-dainty nose. I could feel her warm breath on my face. Intensely, her adoring pale blue eyes looked into mine. She was purring even louder. Her four sets of claws were out instinctively to maintain purchase. But they had gone right through my thin shirt and pierced my soft sensitive skin.

I gasped out silently in pain.

'Arghhh!'

I winced as I used my free right hand to grab Silky by the loose fur at the back of her neck. I was trying to support her weight because if I let her go, for sure she would slide down my chest leaving blood-red track marks in her wake. I knew I wasn't hurting her, but I can assure you she was well and truly hurting me. I barely managed to stop myself from yelling out.

I was in agony as Silky purred on.

And the good lady on the line also purred on.

She continued asking questions and said,

"Yes, I can tell you are in the cattery. I think I can hear a contented cat purring quite close to you."

'I'm sure you can. But what you don't realise is, this cat is not quite close to me, it's on me.'

I was doing my utmost to keep the tension and pain out of my voice. With gritted teeth, I wasn't doing too bad a job of impersonating a ventriloquist with a dummy.

Pleasantly I replied,

"Oh yes, I am just giving Silky her usual welcome cuddle."

But the cuddle Silky was giving me wasn't exactly welcoming at all.

'Cuddle? She's gutting me!'

Silky kept purring, the lady kept talking, I kept on hurting, and the claws kept digging in.

'Please, please. For Christ's sake, get off this phone. I'm bleeding to death here!'

Relentlessly the lady continued,

"With all that purring going on, it sounds like you have got some happy cats in there. I don't think I have any need to view your premises. I want to make the booking with you right now."

'Jesus Christ, this is going to take forever!'

The last thing I needed was a lengthy telephone conversation, which taking details for a pet booking could do. Although I had a pen and paper with me, I told a little white lie to terminate the conversation and, more importantly, my pain.

Here comes the lie,

"I haven't a pen and paper with me to take your details at the moment. I have your number registered on this phone. Can I please call you back?"

She thanked me for my time, which to me seemed like an eternity and without a doubt, it felt like the most extended phone call I had ever received. Indeed, it was the most painful. And Silky was still purring away as I continued to hang onto the scruff of her neck.

With my free hand, I gently unhooked each paw and lifted Silky back onto the shelf. She looked lovingly back at me just as if nothing out of the ordinary had happened. Vacating Silky's run, hugging my chest, I let out an enormous yell of relief,

EEEEEE! AGHHH!

I am sure it was heard miles away.

Right out of the blue, a soft lady's voice said,

"Hello. Are you having trouble in there? Do you need any help?"

'OH NO! Who is that?'

I turned and looked.

I could see a little old lady with silvery-white hair tied up in a bun and wearing bottle-bottom magnifying glasses. She was cautiously peering through the mesh of the security door. I was so embarrassed and wondered what on earth she must have been thinking when she heard my loud yell. Perhaps she thought I had got a tiger in with me. I certainly felt like I had been mauled by one.

My mind raced, and I replied,

"I'll be with you in a minute. I'm just installing a cat called Silky. I've just banged my ankle on Silky's door."

It was amazing what little white lies one could come up with in the heat of the moment.

And that was the second one!

Hurriedly I turned away from my unexpected visitor. I couldn't wait to inspect the skin inside my shirt to find out just how many pints of blood I had lost. Not surprisingly, there were four sets of claw marks with tiny pinprick specks of blood oozing out. Luckily the blood never came through the shirt.

Turning to the lady who looked a little like my Gran, I smiled,

"How can I help you?"

She replied,

"I have heard some excellent reports about your cattery. If you don't mind, I would like to come in and have a look around."

I walked down the cream-tiled path sporting a beaming smile and opened the mesh door to greet her.

As we shook hands, I said,

"Hi, my name is Geoff. Please do come in and meet my friend Silky. She comes to us so often she virtually lives here." (Good sales talk.)

I went into Silky's run, picked her up and cuddled her against my sore chest. She purred as loud as ever.

My Gran look-alike said,

"Oh. How nice. Silky obviously loves you. I can tell you are a cat lover."

'If you had been here three minutes earlier, my darling and read my mind, you might have thought differently.'

She continued,

"Your cattery is so beautiful and clean. I will have no hesitation to board my two cats here."

Producing another proud beaming smile, I replied,

"Oh, thank you very much."

She joked,

"Do you know when I was standing outside the door and heard you cry out in pain, I thought you were keeping lions and tigers in there?"

I burst into laughter.

I looked right into her sparkling eyes and said,

"Oh no, we only accept cuddly cats, just like my friend Silky here."

CHAPTER 6

Temperament?

Here we have some frightening stories, especially the one about Linus. A powerful Tibetan Mastiff.

This chapter is a must-read for budding kennel proprietors, especially if they worry about dangerous dogs.

Because that is exactly what is coming!

To run a business like ours you need all the information you can get about each cat and dog. So, we designed a standard booking form. From the beginning of our business, we used the same booking form throughout. It was a form we designed. We checked out other forms belonging to our opposition. We didn't want anything similar; we wanted our forms to be completely different.

Our booking form was a questionnaire, giving details of the pets that would be staying with us. We had a form for cats and a similar one for dogs. It was obvious they couldn't be the same because they are as different as cats and dogs, excuse the pun.

You would not ask a cat owner,

"Is your cat likely to be in season during their stay with us?"

Equally, we would not ask a dog owner,

"Has your dog been neutered?"

The canine word for doctored is castrated; the feline word for doctored is neutered. Now those two words do bring tears to my eyes!

On the cat-booking form was a very important statement.

NO MALE CATS ARE ALLOWED IN THE CATTERY UNLESS THEY ARE NEUTERED.

Somehow, I do not think the owners of a top-pedigree dog would go for that one!

I must clarify those few points, as it may seem rather strange to some of you why our rules and regulations had to be stipulated.

If a female dog was in season, or likely to come into season, it was always better to be aware of it. We wouldn't want to put her next door to a male dog who would be teased or driven mad with her scent in such a close proximity. For sure, many male dogs would howl their heads off, hoping to get to the female to have their wicked way. No way, did we want to hear lots of howling, or accidentally become a breeding kennel, instead of a boarding kennel. So, it was wise to keep female dogs in season next door to other female dogs and well away from the sensitive noses of the amorous macho males.

Tom cats that haven't been neutered spray their pee everywhere and wow does it smell, or should I say it absolutely stinks. Another point for male cats that aren't neutered is they are generally pedigree cats, which are kept solely for breeding. They are usually owned by people who are running a breeding cattery. If female cats were ready for mating, it made no difference to us, as we had no male cats with testicles in the cattery, unless they were kittens. But more often than not, people tend to have their female cats neutered anyway because they don't want to have their cat getting pregnant while it roams outside its own home.

As we all know, not all cats are pets and many

cats are roaming around our neighbourhoods and countryside, especially tom cats that are semi-wild and not cared for. When tom cats are having their wicked way, they yowl their heads off whilst biting the neck of a female cat. Not unlike bloodsucking vampires. So, when you hear a yowling sound outside your bedroom window in the middle of the night, it is no doubt a tom cat mating. So, if you didn't know before, you do now.

Let us go back to the dog booking form and the title of this chapter, 'TEMPERAMENT!'

What would be your answer if I asked?

"What sort of temperament has your dog got?"

Would your pet be the most placid animal to ever walk this planet?

Is that what you would say?

Would you tell the truth?

Is there a slight chance that your little dog might give us a little nibble on the back of our hand in gratitude for a lovely walk in our beautiful surrounding woodland?

Or, is there a slight possibility that big Bruno might want to rip us into tiny little shreds and swallow the bits if we dared set foot in his kennel?

When filling in the questionnaire some customers were devious and bent the truth, they never informed us that the love of their life could be lethal. Because if they had, they knew their dog would not stand a 'dog in hell's' chance of being accepted into our kennels for one minute.

Let alone two or three frightening weeks!

Ninety-nine per cent of forms that came back accompanied with their deposits were completed in full and by the word, temperament was, friendly, loved to be cuddled, playful, boisterous, or something similar. All these descriptions we had no problem with. Especially loved to be cuddled!

It was the occasional one that gave us the problem, the one that was left blank under the word temperament or read NERVOUS.

NERVOUS?

What the heck is that word, supposed to mean?

I had a look in my dictionary and found out the true meaning of the word nervous. Nervous is a very ambiguous word and it was often used by owners for their dog's temperament. So, what did the dictionary teach me? I will now give you my interpretation of the word, nervous.

The first meaning of nervous was to do with nerves.

Does this mean?

Nervous breakdown?

Or, loss of emotional and mental stability?

Or, does this mean mad dog?

Or, has the dog lost his marbles?

I do not like the sound of that one!

The word also relates to the nervous system in the body, whether it means sinewy or muscular. Well, I have no problem with that explanation; it obviously does not apply to vicious dogs.

The second meaning of nervous uses words like vigorous or terse.

Is the dog vigorous or terse?

Terse sounds a bit dodgy to me!

The third meaning of nervous is described as having disordered or delicate nerves.

I do not like the sound of that one either!

Anyway, after meeting a few of these so-called nervous characters, my nerves have certainly been frayed at times, that's for sure!

Here are a few more words relating to the word nervous.

Excitable... Hey up!

Highly strung... Jesus! Here we go!

Easily agitated... Is that a temperament like a rhinoceros?

Timid... Now I do not mind timid dogs. They are

right up my street, providing they back away. But from my experience, it is the timid ones that are most likely to bite you.

Does that clarify the word nervous for a dog's temperament?

I also decided to check the word ambiguous.

Ambiguous can mean,

Double meaning, doubtful classification, uncertain issue or even obscure.

Could this mean a schizophrenic dog?

I do not like the sound of that one either!

Are you starting to get the picture?

So, when I read the word nervous on the booking form, it certainly made me feel more than nervous.

Let us go back to the first real meaning, good old mad dog, which could also conjure up the word rabid, or psychopath. Now, this word can play tricks with your imagination. Like the Devil's dog or an Alfred Hitchcock movie, relating to a long sharp-pointed knife and blood.

Whose blood?

The dog's blood?

My blood?

My staff's blood?

I am afraid it usually meant my precious blood because if there was an animal that was suspected of being the slightest bit dangerous and with me being the responsible boss, I would be the one to sort the nervous nutter out.

AS ALWAYS, THE BUCK STOPPED WITH ME!

I would never have it any other way.

And yours truly almost getting torn to shreds happened a few times, which I will reveal later.

When we had a nervous dog in, the staff would say,

"Oh no! It's a nervous dog, it could be dangerous.

Get Geoff quick."

So, here are some of my memorable moments with some of my not-so-cuddly canine friends that stepped into my domain. Usually, on their booking forms for temperament, it would be left blank or read...**NERVOUS?**

Mad Lucy

This dog owner, Mr Layton did not try to lie to us, or even bend the truth. Initially, he came to see me and talk about his schizophrenic Golden Retriever bitch called Lucy. Yes, this was a real explanation of a nervous dog which had been diagnosed as schizophrenic.

The poor man was at his wit's end, not knowing what to do with his dog.

I could have told him exactly what to do with it, but I thought better of it.

Over the years I have often been asked,

"What breed of dog would you consider to be the most placid family dog?"

My reply would always be, Labrador, Red Setter, or Golden Retriever. It is a good job we never met any other schizophrenics like Lucy because I would have most definitely crossed Golden Retrievers off my list.

Mr Layton explained that he had owned Lucy from the age of eight weeks when she was a normal cuddly puppy. But, as time went by, her personality drastically changed. When I met Lucy, she was three years old and I might add very lucky to attain that age without being put down.

Lucy was way, way up in the category of highly...

DANGEROUS!

Mr Layton showed me old white scars and some more recent ones on both his arms and on the back of his hands where she had bitten him. He told me he had heard I was a good dog trainer and he wanted to know if we would board her, knowing she was schizophrenic.

He also asked if I could train her, or if I could come up with something to help solve her problem.

I am sure he did not mean shoot her. Or did he?

I pointed out to him that I had no scars on my body.

And I intended to keep it that way!

Being the good soul that I am and not thinking about the boarding and training fees, I agreed to risk my life and try Lucy out for five days and then give him my opinion afterwards.

That is if I was still in one piece!

OR STILL ALIVE!

Mad Lucy was delivered two days later and Mr Layton handed me the lead with her attached to the other end.

Tentatively, I took it.

I bit the bullet and immediately walked her around the wood.

She was okay on the lead, but she had a disconcerting habit...

With her head facing forward, she rolled her eye nearest to me backwards, showing a lot of white, whilst giving me a chilling stare. It sent a shiver down my spine and reminded me of a great white shark.

Mad Lucy's cold stare set my alarm bells ringing, giving me goosebumps and making the hairs stand up on the back of my neck.

'Be careful Geoff. Be very, very careful with this one.'

After the walk with my scary new acquaintance, thankfully I was retaining all my blood. As I entered the kennel-block compound the gate to her run had been left open on my instructions because I wanted to release her lead quickly without her knowing. I must admit I was a bit dubious regarding the outcome. Especially when I released her from the lead.

SUCH AS BEING RIPPED TO SHREDS.

Dubious!

Now that is an understatement if ever, I made one.

I ran Lucy into the run and before she knew what was going on, I released the lead from her collar and quickly stepped out, shutting, and bolting the mesh gate behind me. The moment I let go of her, she spun around and gave me a blood-chilling stare which I will never forget.

GRRRRRRRRRR!

Her name should have been Medusa. I felt I was turning to stone. She certainly sent a freezing chill down my spine that's for sure.

I clipped a large notice on the front of her run.

DANGEROUS DOG TO BE HANDLED BY GEOFF ONLY

During Mad Lucy's five-day stay...HANDLED proved to be the wrong choice of word. She would never let me get anywhere near her again.

She used to give me that same cold Medusa stare as if to say,

"Come in here mate and you won't be going out in one piece!"

I thought cleaning Mad Lucy's run would be an absolute nightmare, but luckily, she didn't like the noise of the power hose or the water that screamed out of the nozzle. So, when I switched on the power hose, she sheepishly slunk away into her sleeping quarters.

Her routine enabled me to close the galvanised steel door of her sleeping quarters while I hosed the run out.

I was very thankful for that small mercy.

Fortunately, she did not fret while staying with us and always ate every morsel of food.

Mr Lawton came to collect her when the five days were up.

I gave him the sad news,

"In my opinion, she should be put to sleep, especially as you have a five-year-old daughter."

Although he had informed me that Lucy had been okay where his daughter was concerned, I thought with Lucy's schizophrenic condition she could turn at any time and I hate to think what would have happened.

Unfortunately, Mr Lawton did not heed my warning.

A few weeks later she bit him quite badly. Reluctantly, he had her put down.

I found all this out because a few months later he brought a lovely yellow Labrador puppy to board with us. That was very good news for him and his family. For me it was double-sided, not only did we get the boarding fees, but we also had a lovely dog with a lovely temperament to look after for years to come.

More importantly, after my encounter with Mad Lucy.

I still had no scars!

Linus The Lion

Does the name Linus conjure up thoughts for a dog's name? Well, to me it sounds more suitable for a lion. Which just happens to be very appropriate for this story.

We had a very large, or a better description would be, a very powerful-looking dog that came to stay with us. A very impressive Tibetan Mastiff.

On his booking form for TEMPERAMENT it read:

PREFERS LADIES

But that left a little bit of a grey area concerning gentlemen, which I am one hundred per cent included in that gender. And because of my self-preservation tendencies, I do not like the sight of my own blood. I thought it would be a very wise idea to clear up the 'grey area' before it turned to 'blood red'.

Meaning mine!

When Linus arrived, I decided to make myself available to sort out the booking form/questionnaire with his owner. Coincidentally, he happened to be called Mr Savage, which turned out to be a very appropriate name for his dog.

Linus Savage.

Believe me, I haven't made these names up!

With Mr Savage sitting in front of me, I quickly looked over Linus's details on the booking form. Almost ignoring everything else that had been filled in. I asked him the sixty-four-thousand-dollar question,

"On Linus's booking form I see against temperament you have put, prefers ladies. Can you be a little bit more specific? Please?"

During the conversation, I was looking at the size of Linus in the back of Mr Savage's car and I hoped it didn't mean...

He prefers ladies to eat!

Mr Savage answered,

"Well, Linus did like men. (What to eat?) But a man accidentally dropped an iron bar on his front foot."

Showing concern I said,

"Wow. That sounds painful."

Mr Savage continued,

"Linus was only five months old when we had builders working on our house. That was when the accident occurred. I took him to the vet to see if anything was broken. The vet concluded that Linus's foot had no broken bones, but was very badly bruised. Unfortunately, the vet was also male and hurt him while examining him. Since that day, Linus has held a grudge against all men. When I take him to the vets, I insist that it is a lady vet who will be tending to him. So apart from me, he just does not like men at all."

I answered,

"Oh, I see."

But I thought differently because I seem to have an affinity with most animals, especially dogs and I was confident I could win Linus over and make friends with him during his two-week stay.

Boy, I could not have been more wrong!

Pat went to get Linus out of the car and take him for his introductory walk. I had never seen such a beautiful dog. He could only be described as magnificent. His dark brown coat glistened in the sun, making his fur look like mink. The hair on his coat was about three inches long and even thicker around his neck. Just like a lion's mane. Hence the name Linus. As he walked, his whole coat swayed. From a distance, apart from his colour, he could have easily been mistaken for a male lion. Considering he was only twelve months old he was enormous and looked very powerful.

I stood outside the office and admired him as Pat walked him by me and he never gave me as much as a sideways glance.

'What an awesome-looking animal.'

The first day I stayed well away from Linus to let him settle in. He took to the girls, no problem at all. The second morning, he happened to brush past me as Jenny one of our girls was walking him back to his run. To my surprise, there was no acknowledgement of my gender.

No acknowledgement at all!

I watched Jenny take him off his lead, stroke him and fuss him before she left his kennel. He appeared to be very placid, so that afternoon with my belief that dogs have an affinity for me, I decided I would take him for his walk around the wood and make friends with him, I wanted to prove to him there were some nice men on his planet.

Is Geoff an idiot, or what?

Anyway, when I stood outside the mesh door to Linus's run, he did not want to know. He barely looked at me as I held his lead in my hand to tempt him for a walk. He just gave me a very sullen look turned his back on me and walked sheepishly into his sleeping quarters. Minutes later I stood and watched as Pat arrived outside his run and she called his name. To my amazement, he bounded straight out to her, just as if nothing had happened.

I might as well have been invisible!

Pat put him on his lead and off they went for a walk. I did take note that he gave me an eerie look as he passed by me.

'Why bother him? He likes the girls.'

'Why risk my neck? Or even the hairs on it.'

The following day one of the girls phoned in sick.

With animals, it is not possible to leave things until the next day. There is a routine that must be followed and all jobs must be tended to, even if we were a person down. So, whenever we were a member of staff short, I would offer to help with the manual work.

Pat usually gave me the task of power-hosing.

The power hose was like a gun with a long lance ending with a nozzle.

Little did I know that the lance was going to save me from horrible injuries.

Or even my life!

When we first started the business, I used to do the power-hosing every day, so it was no stranger to me. I set the power hose up and quickly got back into my old routine. The power hose could easily remove anything which had stuck to the concrete floor of the dog runs, including the most stubborn dog crap, or whatever you would like to call it. I must point out that only a small percentage of our canine guests couldn't wait to go to the toilet until they had their walks in the wood, so not all runs needed to be hosed out every single day. We always shovelled up the dog poo first and then hosed the run down to remove any stubborn debris.

I had completed half the block when I came to Linus's run...

Sinister music started to play in my head.

Was this an inner thought to warn me?

As well as inner thoughts, there was a large card

attached to the outside of his run, it had been put there by Pat in large bold writing.

Coincidentally, in the colour of... BLOOD!

DOES NOT LIKE MEN
ESPECIALLY YOU GEOFF
KEEP OUT!

'Ha-ha. Very funny Pat. I'll show you.'

Cautiously I peered into the big boy's run.

He was nowhere to be seen.

'Maybe he is fast asleep. Do I get one of the girls?'

'Or, do I risk it?'

I only needed a few strides to enable me to close the steel door to his sleeping quarters.

'He who dares wins!'

Tentatively, I slid the bolt of his run trying not to make the slightest sound.

With extreme caution, I tiptoed my way in.

Gingerly, I edged forward.

I reached out to close the steel door...

GRRRRRRRRR!

To my horror...

LINUS CHARGED THROUGH THE ENTRANCE!

'OH NO! I'M DEAD!'

I still had the gun of the power hose in my hand.

It was my only defence.

Instinctively, I pointed it straight at him.

I squeezed the trigger.

It stopped him in his tracks for a moment.

I had a split second.

To get out...

Frantically backpedalling, I backed out.

I slammed the mesh gate.

I should never have been there.

The steel frame of the gate jammed the end of the lance near the nozzle.

It stopped me from closing the gate properly.

Lucky for me...

Linus switched his aggression to the nozzle.

He grabbed it in his mouth.

GRRRRRRRRR!

The nozzle was jetting out water, at a pressure of one thousand eight hundred pounds per square inch.

In his seething temper...

GRRRRRRRRR!

He did not take a blind bit of notice.

'Wow, t*hat nozzle could have been my arm. Or even worse, a much more sensitive part of my body!'*

I released the trigger leaving the gun pinned halfway up the gate.

As soon as the jet of water stopped.

SNARLING...

Linus transferred his aggression toward me.

GRRRRRRRRR!

He reared up on his hind legs and placed his massive paws on the gate.

His head, with jaws snapping, was dead level with my face.

GRRRRRRRRR!

He looked more like a grizzly bear than a dog.

Unbelievingly, his eyes changed from brown to glowing red.

'Jesus Christ!'

His mouth was wide open.

His teeth were barred in a vicious snarl.

He was so close to my face I could feel his hot breath.

GRRRRRRRRR!

'I hope this steel mesh is strong enough to hold him.'

His weight was keeping the gate shut.

He was going ballistic!

He snarled, growled, and chewed at the strong steel mesh.

GRRRRRRRRR!

Blood started to seep from his gums.

'OH NO!'

In his frustrating temper, he was trying to get part of me in his mouth.

He did not care which part.

GRRRRRRRR!

The only good news was...

THE BLOOD...

Was not mine!

I hadn't managed to bolt the gate because I could not get the jammed lance out. I was desperately trying to free it, hoping he would not seize my fingers through the mesh.

If he had, it was most definitely,

GOODBYE FINGERS!

With all the commotion going on, fortunately for me, help arrived in the form of Pat.

She looked me in the eye with obvious disappointment, turned away and simply said in a stern voice,

"Get down Linus, you bad boy!"

The lance came free.

To my amazement, his temper was completely extinguished. It was just as if Pat had turned off a light switch.

Like a naughty chastised child, he walked sullenly back to his sleeping quarters.

One moment Linus was a frenzied beast trying to tear me apart and the next, he was as meek and mild as a lamb.

Pat looked at me and said,

"Have you got a death wish, or what?"

She went into Linus's run and closed the mesh gate behind her. I decided to get out of there while the going was good.

I decided to watch Pat handle Linus from the safety of my office window.

Looking out from the sanctuary of the window. I

just could not believe what I was witnessing!

There was Linus and his lady friend cuddling him in his run. It just did not seem possible to be the same dog from a few minutes before.

Talk about Jekyll and Hyde!

Well, as you can imagine, I stayed well clear of him for the rest of his stay. I decided that he was one animal I was never going to befriend.

On a couple of occasions during Linus's stay, I happened to be near the gate of his run, he growled at me and stared right back into my eyes with a chilling, evil, evil look. His eyes seemed to turn from deep brown to red and they seemed to glow like red hot coals from within the dark brown fur on his face.

Was it my imagination?

I had seen this happen in horror films, but I could not believe it was happening in front of me.

It was just like seeing...

THE DEVIL'S DOG!

I called for Pat to come and witness this unbelievable phenomenon. She arrived in less than a minute and by then his eyes had gone back to brown.

She thought I was pulling her leg.

I said,

"His eyes were definitely changing from brown to red when he looked at me."

Pat gave me a sceptical look.

We stood in front of his run and Sod's Law, his eyes remained brown. He was looking at Pat, completely ignoring me.

I said,

"It is because you are standing here. Go and hide in a kennel where he can't see you and make sure you can see his eyes."

She gave me a knowing look and said,

"Are you joking or what?"

"No, no, no, I am deadly serious. His eyes did change colour. I definitely saw them and I'll prove it to you."

I distracted Linus while Pat went and hid.

I stared into his eyes.

Immediately, he started to growl.

GRRRRRRRR!

It was incredible!

Instantly, his eyes turned red and he had an evil look spread over his face.

Pat shouted from her hiding place,

"I DON'T BELIEVE IT."

Later that week, I discussed the strange occurrence or phenomenon with my vet and even with other vets who used us. None of them had ever heard anything like this before, except in horror movies. I swore it was true. I even had a witness to prove it!

Did Pat and I both witness this phenomenon or did we imagine it?

Linus remained silent.

It was his dark secret.

I ended up having the greatest respect for Linus and felt sorry for him regarding the accident that he had experienced when he was a puppy. Obviously, it had made him mistrust men. Probably until his dying day. The only male person he ever accepted was his owner and I bet my bottom dollar Linus's owner was thankful for that one too.

Fact

A Tibetan Mastiff's height standing on all fours: Males from 30 inches (76 cm) Females from 27 inches (69 cm) Weight: Males about 160 pounds (72 kg). Females are about 150 pounds (68 kg). Tibetan Mastiffs are one of the heaviest breeds of dogs.

A male Mastiff can exceed 200 pounds (90 kg).

That is fifty-five pounds more than me.

No wonder, I was frightened out of my wits!

Tibetan Mastiffs are used in the countries of Tibet, China, Mongolia, and Nepal by local tribes to protect sheep from wolves, leopards, bears, tigers, and large mustelids, (a family of animals, which include weasels, badgers, otters, martens, mink and the ferocious wolverine!).

This story took place in the nineties. I don't know how much Mr Savage paid for Linus, but in 2019, one Tibetan Mastiff fetched $1.5 million. Wow!

More Facts

A Chinese businessman bought a Tibetan Mastiff for a whopping $1.9 million. The reason the dog sold for this high price tag was because it was deemed a 'perfect specimen'. A Tibetan Mastiff with over 95 per cent of breed purity and normal genealogy costs from $2,000 to $3,600. Puppies with good genealogy, have beautiful parents and 99 per cent of breed purity will cost from $3600 to $7000.

A top breeder Zhang Gengyun apparently stated the following about Tibetan Mastiffs,

"They have lion's blood and are top-of-the-range

mastiff studs."

Well, at least I survived Linus to tell the next story...

Killer Kaiser

Here is the next nutter on my list. This nutter was described on the booking form to have a nervous temperament.

He was a large handsome jet-black German Shepherd called Kaiser. And believe me, you do not mess with German Shepherds!

When his lady owner delivered him, she was dressed exceptionally smart and appeared to be in a hurry.

I looked her in the eye.

And came out with my usual line,

"On Kaiser's booking form for temperament, you have written down nervous. Can you be a little bit more specific, please?”

She replied,

“Well, he is nervous.”

"Does that mean he might bite us?"

"Well, he hasn't bitten anyone yet."

'What the heck is that supposed to mean?'

I bit my tongue and kept my thoughts to myself because I did not want to upset her.

In a kind voice, I said,

"If you put him on his lead, I'll get one of the girls to take him for a walk around the wood."

She replied,

"Oh, I don't think that's a very good idea. Kaiser was never walked at the boarding kennels where I left him before."

'Is she trying to tell me something? Or what!'

She continued,

"I would prefer to put him in his kennel myself. That is what they let me do at the other boarding kennel."

'I think I am going to have to take charge of this dog, I can't risk any of my girls with him.'

Reluctantly I said,

"As you wish!"

We never liked the owners putting their dogs straight into the kennels, we preferred taking them for a walk first ourselves so that they got used to us and it helped them to settle down quickly.

Anyway, she had her way.

We put Kaiser's bed in his sleeping quarters and left a clean bowl of drinking water for him. Kaiser's owner put him on his lead and he walked placidly with her to where he would be staying for his two-week duration. You could tell by the way he looked at her, that he thought the world of her.

Fishing, I said,

"I presume he will be okay with us when we walk him?"

She replied,

"I would prefer that if he isn't interested, just leave him alone."

'I don't like the sound of that, one little bit!'

As Kaiser's owner left the car park in a shiny black Jaguar saloon, I looked through the office window. Kaiser was pacing silently up and down his run. I decided to give him half an hour before I went to check him to make sure he was okay.

When I eventually went into the kennel-block, he was in his sleeping quarters.

I called softly,

"Kaiser, come here boy."

Then I had the shock of my life...

With absolutely no warning at all, he came shooting out and launched himself onto his hind legs in a flying fury of black fur and white teeth smashing himself into the gate of his run, just inches from my throat.

I jumped back in sheer...

TERROR!

'At least I am on the outside of the gate!'

The handsome black German Shepherd had turned into probably the most vicious nastiest brute I ever had the misfortune to clap my eyes on. Kaiser made my friend Linus look like a puppy dog. He was attacking the mesh gate with intense fury and aggression as he tried to rip it off its hinges. He was biting the steel mesh so hard that his gums were damaged and bleeding. Pink froth mixed with saliva was erupting from his mouth.

He looked like he had rabies!

The frenzied animal stood on his hind legs for at least twenty minutes non-stop, trying to bite his way out of his new home. No mean feat for a breed that has a profound history of weakness with its back legs.

Every time I or one of the girls went into the kennel-block, Kaiser started again and got himself into an even worse frenzy.

'If this is what he's going to be like, there's no way I am going to keep this animal in here for two hours, let alone two weeks.'

I had no alternative but to ring Kaiser's owner up and ask her to remove him from our premises.

IMMEDIATELY!

As far as I was concerned, he was the most dangerous thing I had ever met on four legs. The frenzied German Shepherd had virtually turned into a vicious wolf. At least Linus could be calmed down by a friendly female.

But for Kaiser, anything human was fair game, no matter what sex it was.

Kaiser's owner arrived in a real panic.

She said,

"I'm catching a plane in five hours. What am I going to do?"

"Why don't you take him to where you boarded him before?"

"Oh, they're full."

'I bet they are. They're just saying that because they don't want your raving lunatic of a dog back with them anymore.'

She looked at me with a very irritated expression and said,

"Oh, I suppose my husband will have to look after him."

Surprised I said,

"Why isn't he looking after him anyway?"

"Oh, sometimes he has trouble handling him and he is away from the house for such long hours. I am the only one who can do anything with him. He is as quiet as a lamb with me."

I gave her one of those Benny Hill looks of amazement. (An English comedian from the seventies and eighties.)

'Oh yes. The truth is really coming out now, isn't it? So that is why you put NERVOUS on his booking

form!'

I could hear Kaiser going ballistic in his run.

Amazingly, as soon as she went into the kennels, he completely changed. It was just like waving a magic wand.

He was yet another Jekyll and Hyde!

Kaiser's owner put him in the car and without saying another word she angrily drove off with tyres squealing. How irresponsible can some people be? That animal was seriously dangerous and that is a gross understatement if ever I heard one. Some of my girls that walked the dogs were only twelve years old. What chance would a young person or even an adult, have against a frenzied attack from Kaiser?

For sure, no chance at all!

His owner said,

"He hasn't bitten anyone yet!"

She never said whether he had devoured anyone though.

In hindsight, I should have refused Kaiser from the very beginning when my alarm bells started to ring. Of course, I wanted the boarding fees, but not at any cost and most certainly not to endanger any of my staff.

Kaiser did not want to just bite us; he wanted to shred us and eat the little pieces as well. I wondered what would have happened if a new customer had come along to view the kennels and as they passed Kaiser's kennel, the nutter had launched himself at them. I am sure it would have almost frightened them to death. And it would be a dead certainty, dead being the operative word here, that they for sure, would not be using our facilities.

Zara

On rare occasions, we accepted a few nervous dogs that could have become dangerous, like our friend Zara. She was quite small for a German Shepherd, but still had the usual set of wolf-like fangs.

In this rare instance, I allowed Zara's owner to take her to her run and she quietly followed him with no hesitation at all. Whenever we went near her run to change her water, give her food, or clean her out, she just shyly slunk into her sleeping quarters.

Zara never wanted to be walked or touched. If we left her alone, she left us alone because she only wanted her privacy. She always ate well, providing we weren't watching her. In fact, she never caused us any problems at all.

Zara came to us for many years right up to the day she died with always the same routine. She died of old age at home.

Sadly, she could never quite overcome her fear of us and just became a little less agitated as the years went by. We all became quite fond of her and felt she wanted to be our friend. When we found out that she had died we were all quite upset. But sometimes, from bad news comes good news and we were delighted when her owners bought a new puppy to stay with us and yes it was a German Shepherd. This time with an excellent friendly temperament.

Over the years, we found out which breeds could generally be classified as the most dangerous and quite a few German Shepherd dogs certainly came high up in that category.

Jack Russells could be a bit feisty but their size helped the situation.

Fact

The Jack Russell takes its name from the Reverend John Russell. He bred one of the finest strains of Terriers for working and flushing out foxes in England.

If the 'Little Jacks' were as large as German Shepherds, they would very likely have been shot on sight. Well, I suppose that is a slight exaggeration by me, by now you should be getting the picture. The cute size of a Jack Russell takes the loss-of-life factor out of the equation.

In fact, we found Dobermans and Rottweilers puppy dogs in comparison to some 'Little Jacks'.

German Shepherds are one of the most intelligent of breeds. They are fantastic family dogs and are so loyal. I know, because I grew up with a German Shepherd named Jassey. I had first-hand experience from an early age of how faithful they are to a family.

Fact

Despite its wolf-like appearance the German Shepherd is a relatively modern breed of dog, with their origin dating to 1899. As part of the 'herding group,' German Shepherds are working dogs developed originally for herding sheep. Since that time, however, because of their strength, intelligence, trainability, and obedience, German Shepherds around the world are often the preferred breed for many types of work, including disability assistance, search-and-rescue, police, military roles, and acting.

Taken out of their environment, German Shepherds can become stressed or frightened and start to protect their new territory, which in our case was their kennel and run.

Some boarding kennels would not accept German Shepherds.

Well, well, what a surprise!

Heidi

Now from big dogs to little dogs, right down to a Miniature Dachshund named Heidi.

Little Heidi was the same colour as a Doberman. In fact, she thought she was a Doberman. Maybe she had seen her reflection in a mirror and with her being the same colour, she had probably imagined herself to be ten times bigger.

And ten times more ferocious!

Miniature Dachshunds do feature Dobermans a little bit, although their legs are considerably shorter.

What a lovely feminine name Heidi is. For me, it conjures up a pretty little Swiss girl with blonde pigtails swishing to and fro as she runs in the sunshine through the spring flowers and green grass on a Swiss mountainside.

Anyway, do not be fooled by that lovely name Heidi. She was a little dog that could pack a punch and a very sly punch at that. Not many dogs came more miniature than Heidi, measuring no more than eleven inches in height.

It was only because of Heidi's size that I decided to take her on. On her booking form under temperament, it read:

FRIENDLY BUT WILL BITE IF SHE CAN GET AWAY WITH IT

That sounded more like a Jack Russell to me!

Well, at least her owners were honest when they filled in the booking form. It seemed Heidi's greatest ambition in life was to bite any fingers that came near her.

Facetiously, I wondered if her owners fed her fingers at home as a little treat now and again.

Hopefully the chocolate variety!

She most definitely had a taste for the pink meaty ones, that's for sure.

Apparently, at Heidi's home, the poor postman was very wary, having experienced a frightening nip when his fingers went too far inside the letterbox. I bet that gave him a surprise.

Well, I can assure you, we did our utmost best to make sure she did not get any of ours!

Heidi visited us many times over the years and was quite a character. She loved to be walked down our woodland path and we got used to handling her with the respect she most certainly deserved. At times it was a challenge or even fun if you can call it that, trying to put her lead on whilst avoiding her small needle-sharp teeth. Then, as we finished the walk, we had to figure out how to take it off again without getting bitten.

On Heidi's gate was a pink card in large blood-red writing:

DANGEROUS LITTLE DEVIL WILL
TRY TO NIP YOU IF SHE CAN!

During dog walking when we went into Heidi's run to put her lead on, she came running toward us looking very friendly, with her undocked black curved tail raised in the air wagging furiously. Now, believe me, if we didn't watch what we were doing, she would have preferred our fingers, instead of her walk. We had to treat her a bit like a dangerous ferret, by quickly grabbing her collar at the back of her neck and then gently lifting her. This suspended her onto her back legs, giving her less manoeuvrability. Then we were able to clip the lead onto her collar as we kept our fingers well and truly out of her way. But the crafty little devil still attempted to twist around to try and bite us.

During the walk, Heidi was 'as happy as Larry' and would let us stroke her back and fuss her. But on her return, it was a different kettle of fish. She thanked us by trying to nip us as we took the lead off. At least taking her off the lead was less risky than putting her on. To unclip her, we suspended her onto her hind legs. But it was virtually guaranteed that the moment her front feet touched the ground she would spin around and we would hear her teeth click, as her jaws snapped together searching for our meaty fingers.

I do not recall if she ever managed to get a hold of any of us, but I can assure you, it wasn't through her lack of trying.

Fortunately, Heidi never seemed to be too interested in biting any other parts of our body during dog walking. Occasionally, when we were cleaning her out, she did go for our ankles, but that was only if she could manage to sneak up from behind. She also developed a habit of running at us yapping like mad, if we stamped our feet and shouted, "NO," she would do a rapid U-turn and run back twice as fast.

One day, little Heidi frightened a young new member of staff and cornered her in the run. The poor girl was terrified. Luckily, help was near at hand from Pat. With a broom in her hand, she pushed the little devil away and no harm was done.

Over the years we got to know Heidi's little moods and tantrums but always found it quite an exciting challenge. No one ever dared attempt to pick her up to give her a loving cuddle, as her owners did.

We all preferred to retain our fingers instead!

Fact

Dachshunds or Sausage Dogs were bred in Germany for hunting badgers. They are courageous and a perfect shape to enter a badger set.

Tanya

Another little dog which had NERVOUS printed on the booking form definitely came in the category of dangerous. Tanya was a Chihuahua. Yes, a dangerous Chihuahua. Can you believe that?

Do you realise how tiny a Chihuahua is?

Fact

Chihuahuas generally range in size from 6 to 9 inches (15 - 23 cm) at the shoulder and weigh anywhere from 3 to 6 pounds (1.3 – 2.7 kg). However, some Chihuahuas can reach up to 15 inches (38 cm) at the shoulder. Breed standards generally do not recognise Chihuahuas that weigh more than 6 pounds (2.7 kg).

Tanya's owners, Mr and Mrs Stevens a pleasant elderly couple were sitting in front of me in my office.

I said,

"I see on the booking form you have written nervous under temperament. What do you mean by nervous?"

Mr Stevens replied,

"Well, Tanya is likely to bite, but it shouldn't be a problem, because of her size."

'No problem! For who? The dog or us?'

Anyway, I decided to trust my intuition and I took Tanya on.

What could possibly go wrong?

Subsequently, we found out that if Tanya had been big enough, she would have ripped us to bits.

We soon realised why the so-called nervous dogs came to stay with us. You can't ask your next-door neighbour to look after *'Rover'* when it's more than likely that *'Rover'* would put him or her into hospital or even an early grave.

If we had known about Tanya's nasty nature, I can guarantee we would never have let her set a paw on the premises. We had great difficulty looking after her because of her tendency to be rather violent toward us. If we went into her territory, we had to be armed with a large bass broom to protect us from being savaged. And this is only a Chihuahua I am describing. The broom head was much larger than her, but that did not stop her from biting it in temper. With the broom head, we gently pushed her back into her sleeping quarters and then locked her in enabling us to clean the run. We felt a little bit like a lion tamer with a whip and a chair, but we were missing the whip and the broom sufficed as the chair.

With a diminutive Chihuahua, you might think taking a broom to her was perhaps a little bit over the top. But I can assure you with Tanya it was an absolute necessity. With Tanya being so ultra-quick we had to walk out backwards, dragging the broom on the floor of the run in-between us and her, because her favourite form of attack was from behind. Mind you, I suppose you couldn't blame her for a sneaky rear attack, considering the size of a Chihuahua to a human being. I certainly wouldn't contemplate tackling a creature that is more than twenty times bigger than me. Would you?

Sadly, Tanya was one of the few dogs that died on

our premises. Over the years, it was inevitable an occasional death would occur when dealing with literally thousands of cats and dogs.

Early one morning, one of the girls found Tanya lying in a pool of blood. The blood appeared to have come from one of her ears. It was a tremendous shock for the young girl to find the little dog in that condition. According to our vet, Tanya's death was caused by a terminal brain tumour, which apparently had been there for some considerable time at least it was no fault of ours. No wonder the poor tiny dog was so violent. A dog cannot tell you it has a headache; let alone the extreme pain it would be suffering with a brain tumour.

That was obviously why Tanya had a nervous temperament, or should I say, in her case, an extremely violent one.

We had never dealt with a death on the premises before and I was unsure what the procedure should be. I decided to have Tanya's body kept at the vets in a freezer, just in case Mr and Mrs Stevens wanted to take it for burial, or maybe want a second opinion.

I was dreading telling them. As I mentioned before, they were quite elderly.

I did not want to phone them while they were away because I could not see the point in spoiling their holiday. And there was nothing they could do anyway. All I could do was wait for Tanya's dreaded collection day and phone them before they left home and finally break the sad news. I thought it would give them time to come to terms with their sad loss before they arrived to collect Tanya. I certainly did not want them turning up in a post-holiday mood, only to be told that their little Tanya was in the vet's fridge. Not only would it have been devastating for them, but it would not have been a very good advert for our business, especially if we had customers in the office listening to the fact that a dog had just died in our care.

I could just have imagined the scene.

Tanya's owners would be in my office sobbing and crying their hearts out, and other customers would be thinking,

'Jesus, they let dogs die in here. It could be a bit dodgy using this place.'

Of course, the other customers wouldn't be listening to the full story of how Tanya had died, just the fact that she was dead and I mean well and truly dead. Bad rumours spread rapidly and it might not have been too long before our premises became taboo when it was certainly no fault of our own.

I have always believed it can take years to build up a good reputation and five minutes to destroy it.

On the day that Tanya was to be collected, I was not looking forward to the phone call one little bit. I decided to make the call from our cottage rather than the office. Again, I did not want any customers overhearing me and getting the wrong impression.

I rang their house many times and eventually made contact just before they left for our premises. They were heartbroken and in no way held us responsible for Tanya's demise. They insisted on paying for Tanya's full stay, even though I suggested we did not want any money at all. But they were adamant and paid the full fifteen days.

Again, good news followed bad because the following year they booked Tanya's successor. The new dog was a puppy named Tara and she was a Chihuahua as well. Her temperament said friendly and that was exactly how she was. She liked to be picked up and cuddled. Now that is the type of dog we really liked.

As the business progressed, if the description for the word temperament was vague, either my manager or I would carefully vet them. If there was any doubt whatsoever that the owner could not be specific about the temperament, we would refuse to take their dog. It wasn't worth the risk.

To give you budding kennel owners some piece of mind, it was only a small percentage that we refused.

We certainly did, 'live and learn' as the saying goes.

And I am still here with no scars to prove it!

It might sound a bit like running a boarding kennel is a form of business where you risk your life almost every day. Well, it's not quite as bad as it sounds, because dangerous dogs were few and far between. I would say there was less than one percent of dogs that came to us over the years in that dangerous category. And as I mentioned earlier, we boarded thousands.

We just made sure, we thoroughly checked out those ambiguous words that were put on the booking form, for describing that word...

TEMPERAMENT!

CHAPTER 7

Are Rottweilers Aggressive?

Taz And Fritz

A tale of two GIANTS.

Having survived the temperament chapter with me, you might wonder what is coming next.

Are Rottweilers aggressive?

Well, some Rottweilers can be aggressive, but generally, they are a much-maligned breed, probably because they are portrayed in movies and TV series as being aggressive guard dogs. I must admit, I had no experience with Rottweilers before we had our business so my knowledge about this breed was virtually zero.

ALL I KNEW WAS THEY COULD BE POTENTIALLY DANGEROUS!

The very first booking I took for a Rottweiler wasn't for one but for two of the fearsome-looking monsters. Their names were Taz and Fritz and their owner's name was Mr Charles. It was with a little bit of trepidation that I took the booking, well actually a lot of trepidation.

At the appointed time, Mr Charles pulled into our carpark in a green Range Rover. To my consternation, I noticed that the suspension was heaving up and down and I could just make out the shapes of two giant heavyweights representing Taz and Fritz who appeared to be jumping up and down in their keenness to get out.

Looking at the size of them, I sincerely hoped it was for a walk...

And not to get at me!

As I was checking the Rotties vaccination certificates, Mr Charles, proudly informed me that their combined weight was two hundred and forty pounds.

CAN YOU BELIEVE IT TWO HUNDRED AND FORTY POUNDS!

Well, I certainly believed it, as I looked at the huge hounds. The two giant Rottweilers were lumps of solid muscle, teeth, and fangs. To my mounting concern, they were looking directly at me who was weighing in at only one hundred and forty-seven pounds. I thought I would need help because there was no way I could manage the two giants on my own.

I had a consoling thought,

'If Pat helps me, at least I will not be dying alone.'

But Mr Charles insisted I would be able to manage them and said,

"Don't worry Mr Doody, my wife always walks them. You will have no problem at all."

'I'm going to die for sure.'

Well, it was all right for him to say that his wife walked them, but they had no idea who the heck I was. I just hoped he couldn't see that I was more than a little dubious.

A little dubious is a serious understatement if ever I made one!

Their wide collars were made of black leather with dull silver studs. This made the two brutish-looking dogs appear more fearsome than ever. Mr Charles struggled to hook their leads onto their collars as they bounded and pounded about in the back of the Range Rover.

At that moment I would have given a million pounds to change them into miniature Poodles. Stuff what my macho friends think about me walking toy dogs because I can assure you that toy dogs were growing on me by the second!

Eventually, they were attached to their collars and that made them bark louder than ever as they spit saliva all over themselves and their owner in their excitement to go for a walk.

Hopefully not a meal.

Meaning me!

So, I prepared to meet my maker as the two leads were handed to me.

WAS I NERVOUS OR WHAT!

But I had no choice, so off the three of us jolly well went.

'Is this going to be the last time I would ever be seen alive?'

I certainly hoped the enormous Rotties didn't sense my fear. And at that stage of the proceedings, my underwear was still clean.

And I hoped it was going to remain so!

I hadn't been walking the two monsters for long, when it suddenly dawned on me that I was still alive and kicking and as a bonus, in one piece as well!

Taz and Fritz didn't pull on their leads one little bit; in fact, they were quite gentle and even seemed to like me and I realised I was enjoying myself.

'PHEW!'

I didn't get ambushed in the woods and torn to shreds after all.

When I miraculously returned without the slightest scratch on me, I had made friends with two of the loveliest-natured Rottweiler gentlemen one could ever meet. I could tell they liked me and I thought they were great, in fact, they were fantastic. As I installed my two new mates in their temporary home, they didn't act anything like the ferocious breed they portrayed.

And with them behaving so gently, they were more like lambs.

During Taz and Fritz's stay, there was only one problem we had with the gentle giants. The problem materialised when potential customers came to inspect the kennels.

When they were in their run Taz and Fritz were normally very quiet and would lie sprawled out calmly watching the girls go about their daily chores. But on spotting strangers, meaning visiting potential customers, they changed into roaring lions. Barking like crazy and spitting slobber, they got up on their hind legs which raised them to a height of over four feet. A truly frightening spectacle! The staff knew they weren't dangerous and only wanted to protect their territory. But potential customers did not realise that one little bit as the Rotties' apparent aggression almost frightened the crap out of them.

Causing a coronary would be a more appropriate description!

Who could blame newcomers for thinking that Taz and Fritz wanted to rip their heads off? The two Rotties never made a murmur when any of us entered the kennels, it was just when they saw a stranger.

Well, there is one thing I know for sure, I wouldn't want to be a burglar in their house!

The potential customers might have thought if they boarded their miniature pooches here with Taz and Fritz behaving in such a ferocious way, they could have frightened their little dogs to death. Or even eaten them!

Also, there was no way I wanted to get sued for a customer dropping dead on our premises.

The problem was solved by shutting Taz and Fritz in their sleeping quarters before inviting customers for an inspection. The two giants were then as quiet as church mice and when prospective customers took their time walking around, little did they realise what muscle, teeth and power was lurking behind that galvanised door.

Taz and Fritz stayed with us dozens of times and it was to our utmost pleasure that we met two gentle German giants.

On reflection, we wouldn't have missed that wonderful experience for the world!

CHAPTER 8

Pure Unadulterated Mayhem

The caricature depicts that there were many days when it felt like it was raining cats, dogs and customers.

This chapter gives an insight into running a very busy pet hotel with a bit of my humour added.

The title of this chapter describes a typical delivery and collection day on one of our August weekends. It is also a good description of many other busy days...

Pure mayhem!

No Room At The Inn?

After a few years, when we were well established. We could have as many as seventy cars arriving in one day. Cats and dogs were either being delivered or collected. On those busy days, we used to try and space the customers out with pre-arranged appointments. We did this by asking each customer to fill in a booking form where the date and time of delivery or collection were written and signed. And in most cases, booking forms were completed months in advance. When the customer finally arrived on our premises on the correct date, the pre-arranged times had been well and truly forgotten. Or maybe totally ignored! Therefore, the whole lot came during the same hour instead of half the customers arriving in the morning and half in the afternoon. So, you may now be able to picture the pure mayhem which we endured.

Customers delivering had schedules and deadlines to meet, a typical example being trains, boats and planes. Of course, they would be excited because, in most cases, they were going on their annual holidays.

We would say,

"We had you down as delivering at 11 am this morning?"

They would reply,

"Sorry, I forgot. I didn't think it would matter anyway."

Or...

"Oh, we decided to hang on to '*Rover*' (the dog), or '*Tiddles*' (the cat), until the last minute."

Or...

"The cat had noticed the suitcases the night before and did a disappearing act. He didn't like the idea of us leaving him behind. It took us hours to catch him."

The fact is, the same customer's cats did the vanishing trick every year. So why on earth didn't they just keep them in the night before? That would be a sure way to prevent the crafty cat from disappearing over the horizon. So, it was often their next-door neighbour who delivered the offending cat the next day. For sure, there was never a dull moment in this trade.

Inevitably, all the customers who turned up at the same time wanted attention immediately.

Now that is what you call mayhem…Pure Mayhem!

Customers delivering were generally in a hurry because they were running late and customers collecting their loved ones missed them and wanted to see them as soon as possible. So, cats were arriving and leaving the cattery at a fair rate of knots, and dogs were doing likewise at the kennels. I imagined all this chaos was just like running a hotel business. The only difference was our guests could not speak and tell their owners (hence the title of this book) what an excellent time they were going to have or what an excellent time they had. Such as my mate Skip trying to commit suicide on the A41. Well, this impediment did have one distinct advantage, because the guests couldn't complain if they had had a bad time, although I can't envisage any of our furry guests not enjoying our five-star facilities.

The major disadvantage of not being able to talk to our guests was when their owners were late by a day or two.

We couldn't say to our furry guests,

"I'm sorry, your room is booked. You will have to find accommodation elsewhere."

If this situation arose, as it did many, many times. What could we do? Well, the easiest solution was to tie the kennel-less dog to one of the trees in the wood and release the cats into the surrounding countryside, where I am sure they would have the time of their lives hunting the abundant wildlife. But I am afraid life was not that simple, especially with us being responsible pet carers. Of course, we had to hang on to them or face the wrath of their doting owners. So, we had no choice.

To get through the problem, we had to move our guests around here, there, and everywhere. Meaning in extreme emergencies boarding up to five cats in our cottage, with (hopefully) clean habits. They were our guests in different rooms, such as the utility, storeroom, and spare bedrooms. Our bedrooms? Now that is what you call five-star luxury!

In these emergencies, we used the office, the staff toilet, the clipping room and the kennel kitchen. Also, we put dogs in our garage and even in our private kennels. The three private kennels were situated under an eighty-year-old oak tree near the end of our garden. They housed my three liver and white English Springer Spaniels, Sally, Jess and Jemma. (You will meet Sally in later stories.) This resulted in the three of them briefly sharing one kennel. It wasn't a problem because they got on well. In fact, they were related, Sally was the mother of Jess and Emma. We got by any which way we could, but sometimes it would only be by the skin of our teeth.

I will never forget this classic story.

On a mega-busy day, with the car park full and the office overflowing with customers, we had a new lad helping us with the dog walking and bathing. He had only been with us for just over a week and had been a great help. He will remain nameless!

He was walking past the office empty-handed. I called him and asked him to take care of a new dog named Jake that had just arrived. I handed him Jake's lead with the excited Jake securely attached, he took him for the introductory walk around the wood. With me being so busy, I completely forgot about him and Jake.

About twenty minutes later, I saw him standing with Jake outside the office window, looking lost and nervously peering in.

To my horror, he shouted at the top of his voice,

"I HAVE WALKED AROUND ALL THE KENNEL BLOCKS, AND I CAN'T FIND AN EMPTY ONE TO PUT THIS DOG IN!"

The bombshell effect was like throwing a switch. The reaction in the office teeming with noisy customers changed the bustling atmosphere to deadly silence. You could have heard a pin drop. Every customer turned and looked at the forlorn lad with his new dog.

Customers who had brought a dog with them for boarding must have been thinking,

'OH NO! There is no room at the Inn. What are we going to do?'

So, what do you do in a situation like that?

Well, my first thoughts were obvious.

A very easy solution.

'Shoot the boy!'

But that was not going to solve our massive problem.

Was it?

It only lasted a few seconds, but the silence seemed to make time stand still for a lifetime. Kathy and I looked at each other, our eyes open wide with disbelief. Thinking quickly, I excused myself as politely as possible and gently parted a space between the queue of deathly quiet customers. Just like Moses parting the sea! I rushed out of the office to get to the lad (with thoughts of strangling him) before he had a chance to utter one more embarrassing word.

I said to him in a very calm and confident tone, just loud enough for all our customers to hear,

"Oh yes, we do have some free. There are kennels vacant in number four-block. With you being new, somehow you must have overlooked them. Please follow me with Jake."

Before the lad had a chance to reply, I whisked him and the bemused Jake away, leaving poor harassed Kathy to the office mayhem. I just had to sound confident in front of all those customers because I knew there would be plenty of kennels available later in the day. We just had to stall for time. As soon as I got the lad inside kennel block four, (the furthest point away from customers as possible) I explained what he should or should not say in front of an office full of customers.

To his credit, the new lad had tried hard to please us during the week, and I certainly did not want to upset him. I explained in the best possible way that he must never come back to the office with a dog and say there is nowhere to put it, especially in front of thousands of customers. Well, that was a slight exaggeration, for sure not quite thousands, but maybe twenty or thirty. I told him that in future, he must stay at the back of the kennels with his charge and wait for a more experienced member of staff, who would eventually come and take care of the situation.

But the problem remained. Where is the dog going to go?

I sent the lad and Jake around the wood again. Jake was more than happy to go for another walk, his tail wagging in excitement.

With the lad and Jake temporarily out of the way, I worked out what to do in the embarrassing situation. I solved the problem of no room at the inn by temporarily shutting a placid black Labrador guest in her sleeping quarters, leaving space for the new dog in the vacant run.

I must add, when a customer was unfortunate enough to be delayed, we had to work our way around it because we had no choice, but I must say, it never upset any of the dogs.

Bedding

Another big problem we had to contend with was the heaps and heaps of bedding that owners brought in for their dogs. It was not a problem with cats because their owners usually brought them a woollen jumper to sleep on, but dog bedding was an absolute nightmare. Why? Well, the answer is, the owners brought in truckloads of the stuff. In the case of Great Danes, we accepted and used mattresses provided by their owners. The fact is, Great Danes, need a comfortable mattress to protect them from their heavy bones rubbing on a hard surface resulting in bed sores. Great Danes spend many hours lying down, unlike other breeds that jumped around like 'Jack-in-the-boxes' most of the time. I am sure you remember, my mate Boisterous Ben in the second chapter.

Miniature poodles and other small dogs didn't need a big mattress, which would be better suited for human beings. But the owners still insisted on bringing them. They fetched bean beds, soft beds, feather beds, not forgetting dozens of pillows with all sorts of fillings. Plastic beds, wicker baskets, beds filled with polystyrene, deck chairs and even in one case…

Can you believe?

A large brown leather armchair!

They brought blankets, sheets, eiderdowns, and duvets. You name it. We stored it. Yes, stored it, because most of the bedding was unsuitable for use in a boarding kennel. We explained that we had our own bedding, especially designed and made for boarding kennels. But would they, have it? No, of course, they wouldn't. They insisted that 'Rover' had to sleep on unaccustomed luxury. We informed them that it would be ruined by the mud from the woodland walk. In the end, to make them happy, we took it, said nothing, and stored it.

We had a large industrial washing machine for standard-sized dog bedding, but no way could we wash barrow loads of duvets.

Can you imagine this scenario? It is pouring down with rain, and '*Rover*' is walked along our peaty woodland path. What would a spotless pink duvet look like after twenty-four hours? What sort of state do you think '*Rover*'s' bedding would be in after two or three weeks? For sure, it would be unrecognisable and completely ruined as well.

Often when owners were delivering the bedding, they would say,

"It does not matter how dirty it gets. I would prefer you to use it."

But I am certain that if we had given their bedding back, filthy and smelling vile, it would most definitely have mattered. And give us a bad name to boot.

So, we labelled everything that they brought, so that when it was collected, it would be nice and clean. And dear old '*Rover*' would not have missed it one little bit. Instead, he would have been sleeping quite comfortably on one of our more than adequate (look-alike) beige sheepskin mats, which we could easily wash during and after his stay.

Our bedding stories sound as if we were quite sensible, but we did learn the hard way. At the start of the business, in our naivety, we let dogs sleep on whatever their owners brought. Experience with bedding proved to be a big learning curve, or should I say, an absolute nightmare. On many occasions, we found out in the morning just what our mischievous canine guests had been up to during the night.

'*Rover*' would be wagging his tail with a proud look on his face as if to say,

"Hey Geoff, look what I have done. Aren't I a clever boy?"

Good old '*Rover*' would be standing up to his chest in bed fillings. It could have consisted of anything from feathers, foam, polystyrene and even the beans out of a bean bag. Can you imagine how long it took us to clear that lot up, chasing feathers and such all over the kennel blocks? And what about the bedding soiled with pee and crap? I can assure you, not for the faint-hearted or even the most patient person in the world.

After '*Rover*' had savaged his bed in one of his frenzies of fun, we tried to explain to the not-very-amused owners why he had done such a thing. Most owners never seemed to understand and would often say something like,

"Well, he never does anything like that at home."

'I know he does not do it at home, but this isn't his

home. This is a boarding kennel!'

The reasons why '*Rover*' chewed up his bedding or went to the toilet on it, in it or under it, could have been multitudinous. He might have been fighting canine battles in his dreams, or just playing, or even just a little bored, or perhaps he felt like being a little bit naughty. Who knows why the dogs did it? All I know is, it certainly wasn't stress because they always stood there wagging their tails, feeling rather pleased with themselves and looking up at you as if to say,

"Come on, bring the next one. I will show you just how fast I can rip it into shreds."

In those hectic times, the precious bedding that we meticulously labelled and stored was mountainous. Unfortunately, the occasional label fell off. When this happened, it created great confusion when the owners came to collect it. After a lot of time-consuming searching, it was unfortunate, because sometimes we could not find it.

For us, it was standard procedure to issue a pink card for a female dog and a blue card for a male dog. We clipped it on every gate to each run and wrote the dog's name and leaving date. Underneath the names and dates, we wrote any other relevant information, including bedding stored. This procedure meant we had information about the stored bedding twice, labelled in the storeroom and written on their kennel card, so nothing could go wrong.

But occasionally, it did!

I will never forget one chap who came to collect Goldie, (a very popular name for this breed) his lovely Golden Retriever on a busy Saturday. Goldie had been staying with us quite happily for three weeks. He paid his bill and was extremely pleased with her as she came out of the kennels in tip-top show-dog condition with her golden coat shining in the sun. He asked for Goldie's beige blanket, so I sent one of our girls, Caroline, to retrieve it from the storeroom. But she returned with disturbing information. There was no beige blanket anywhere. So, I sent her off to search a second time amongst the mountainous heaps of clean bedding. She also checked Goldie's kennel and others nearby. Alas, that beige blanket was nowhere to be seen. It had disappeared off the face of the earth. The office was full of customers as the blanket-less chap just stood there getting redder in the face by the minute with his arms folded across his chest for at least twenty minutes.

My thoughts were,

'Is it his blanket or the dogs?'

I think he must have been a bit short of blankets in his house, or this one had got a gold thread running through it. As we took care of at least a dozen customers, he huffed and puffed like a bad advert. I thought it was about time I solved the situation, one way or another.

I said with a concerned look,

"I am, very sorry, we can't find it. Maybe it has gone out with another customer. So, sorry it is our mistake. How much do you think the blanket is worth?"

He mumbled,

"I don't know."

"Well, would you accept this ten-pound note for the blanket? I will ask my manager on Monday if she knows where it is, or what could have happened to it. If we do find it, I will post it to you and please keep the ten pounds."

He reluctantly accepted my offer and drove away obviously not a happy chappy.

After the disgruntled chap left blanket-less, another customer waiting to be attended to made a very memorable statement,

"Well, what a Pratt. He seemed to be more interested in the blanket than his dog."

'What can I say?'

I sighed,

"Yes, I know it seems crazy, doesn't it?"

We never did find his beige blanket. We had no idea what could have happened to it. Sadly, we never saw Goldie again.

As they say, 'There is nought as queer as folk'.

Food

We had a few customers who went a bit over the top with their instructions on how we should care for their cats or dogs. Their list of instructions was endless, to coin a phrase, 'as long as your arm' . We had heard or read many requests from hundreds of different customers many, many times before. So, nothing was new to us anymore. However, we had to humour them and listen patiently for precious minute after minute as they insisted on reading everything to us, even though they left the list with us anyway.

So, biting our tongues, we politely waited for them to finish their long list of explicit instructions, which would often be in front of a large queue of customers. We could see the queuing customers starting to roll their eyes and get more and more agitated by the second. To me, it was understandable because the waiting customers were probably on a very tight schedule.

A customer might say,

"Please do not feed '*Rover*' until precisely five

o'clock, or he won't touch his food."

'*Rover*' obviously carried a watch with him!

The fact was, as soon as we fed '*Rover*' at our usual time of four o'clock, he would wolf it down not unlike a vacuum cleaner. He probably thought that he had competition from other dogs he could see in the runs on either side of him or the row opposite.

Dogs boarding with us had no idea or imagination that the dogs that they could see were not able to get to their food. Owners did not realise that dogs do not think or act the same when living in a boarding kennel as they do at home. It was also common sense that two dogs sharing from the same family home would need to be separated when fed. This was just in case they got jealous and wanted to rip their best canine friend to bits if he or she attempted to steal its food. So, for sure, we took every precaution.

Can you imagine one dog saying to the other?

"You're not having any of my food mate. You come near it, and you're going to die."

Also, we needed to know if dogs sharing a kennel had eaten their own food because it could have been a different type or a special diet or even included medication. No way could we stand there and watch each pair finish eating. We were just too busy. So, of course, they had to be separated for that short period. One in the sleeping quarters and one in the run. But the lists kept coming and coming, informing us of all the obvious things that we had seen so many times before.

Not only did we get a full list of instructions for some canine guests, but we also had mountains of exotic food the owners had brought in for us to contend with. Preparing all the dog food could be a nightmare. At feeding time, the kennel kitchen had row after row of stainless-steel bowls (sometimes well over one hundred), all with different types of food filled to the brim.

When the kennels were chock-a-block, sorting all the different diets could take one member of staff almost all day to prepare. During the week, it was usually the manager and Kathy at weekends. What a job it was. Of course, I did it in the beginning, but in the latter years, because I had a lot of maintenance, it was one chore I was quite happy to stay away from. The bowls had to be set out in a particular order for the different types of food and medication. When all the food had been prepared there were rows and rows of glistening stainless-steel bowls. It looked very much like a chef from a top London hotel had prepared it. You had to see it to believe it. On reflection, I should have taken some photographs of the impressive scene. Well, I am not really into dog food, but some of it looked pretty tasty to me.

At least twenty per cent of owners provided food for their cats and dogs. This could vary considerably. There was fresh chicken, turkey, beef, ham, prawns, fish, rice, vegetables, cheese, you name it, they fed them on it.

I never witnessed any curry!

We also cooked food that caring owners had brought in. Not only was it very time-consuming, but the lingering smell wasn't always pleasant. But '*Tiddles*' or '*Rover*' must have their regular diet. There are numerous pet food brands, and we did not stock everything, even though we had a large storeroom capable of storing lorry loads of the stuff. Rather than change their diet, which could cause all sorts of problems such as stress meaning upset stomachs, accompanied by the dreaded diarrhoea, we insisted on owners bringing their pets regular food and reduced their bills accordingly.

The last straw for me was when we had three cats for two weeks and Kathy had stacks of raw fish to cook daily in the kitchen of our cottage. For me, the smell was awful, and yuk, it lasted for hours afterwards. Unfortunately for me, I am not too fond of the smell of fish, having previously skinned and gutted them for eight years in the family fish and chip business.

So that was it. I went out and bought a large microwave for the kitchen at the kennels.

As they say,

"Where there's a will, there's a way."

In the latter years, we asked for certain foods to be precooked and put into freezer bags for each day.

Medication And Geoff's Frightening Phobia

Well, all that information about bedding and food was a profound insight into how we ran our pet hotel. The saga goes on because not only did we have all the special diets to contend with, we also had some pets on medication, which could include injections administered daily.

Now that is where squeamish me drew the line.

No way was I giving injections!

Unfortunately, from a very early age, I have had a massive phobia of injections. I had horrendous imaginative thoughts such as, what if I slipped and stuck the needle in myself and not the dog? It just does not bear thinking about.

The injections were administered by the manager or Kathy. They, by the way, didn't have my phobia, and Kathy was even a blood donor. To my mind, those awful syringes are taboo. I must admit to overwhelming nausea coming over me, even at the thought of them.

'Arghhh!'

That, thankfully, is my only phobia.

I cannot resist butting into the cat and dog stories to tell you how my phobia is now virtually cured.

Or should I say, it is most certainly a heck of a lot better!

So, here comes some humour.

Story number one

One day at school, when I was only twelve years old, I was called to the front of the class by my maths teacher, Mr Jeff Turner who was a lovely man. Unfortunately, he was quite deaf and wore a hearing aid, so we kids cruelly nicknamed him, 'Deaf Geoff'. It surprised me when Mr Turner handed me a letter informing me that I was to have an injection to prevent polio, a terrible crippling disease. As I read the letter, my phobia was so bad, I passed out like a light and fell into his arms slipping against his blazer pocket. Unfortunately, his fountain pen was lurking there and it stabbed me in the chin. That was an ink injection that I will never forget. Now that has got to be a first. I will guarantee most of you younger readers are thinking. What the heck is a fountain pen?

As medication progressed, children were far luckier than my generation because the polio vaccine was a sugar lump on the tongue, not a dreaded injection.

Story number two

When I was in my late teens, my father recited a hilarious memory when I was only three years old. This event took place at the local clinic.

Father and little me were holding hands in a cold long corridor in a queue of crying children. Like me they were terrified. We were queuing for vaccinations for diphtheria. The injection was to be administered by a plump stern-looking Sister dressed in grey and white with a matching nurse's hat. When my father and I shuffled closer to the relentless Sister who was holding a great big syringe in her hand (to me it looked two feet long). Father decided to take off my jacket and slipped my right arm out of the sleeve in readiness for the penetration of my delicate young skin. With my eyes wide open in sheer terror and seeing Sister's monstrous needle getting nearer and nearer I realised that it would soon be my turn for the incoming torture. I was even more terrified when he took my left arm out of the other sleeve. As he held my jacket, my arm had barely left the sleeve when I decided this wasn't for me...

I ran for my life!

Like a bolt of lightning, I shot straight down the corridor and hot-footed it right out of the clinic, leaving my father holding an empty jacket.

Story number three

Many years later, I am not going to say how many. I had an appointment with my doctor, Dr Handley. I had known him for many years, and we were on quite friendly terms. I really liked his dry sense of humour which is relevant to this third story.

He said the dreaded words,

"Geoff, I think you need to have a blood test."

Mortified I said,

"When?"

With a sadistic smile on his face, he said,

"Today! Meaning now!"

Even more mortified, I blurted out,

"OH NO!"

Starting to show some sympathy for my terrifying plight, he said,

"Don't worry Geoff. I know you don't like needles, so instead of Sister performing the blood test, I will do the job myself."

I do not like needles. Was that a gross understatement, or what?

I WAS ABSOLUTELY TERRIFIED OF THEM!

Scared out of my wits and feeling like I was facing a firing squad, reluctantly I followed him to a small room, (torture chamber). I was trying to be as brave as possible for a grown man. As instructed, acting a darn sight braver than I felt, I lay on a white surgical couch and rolled up my right sleeve. As I did so, I spotted a packet of sweets sitting on the shelf opposite. I recognised them as Rowntree Jelly Babies. They were and still are one of my favourites. Then I had a brilliant idea...

Licking my lips in anticipation, I said,

"Is there any chance of one of those sweets Doc?"

He gave me one of his typical answers,

"You can have the complete packet for all I care."

With no hesitation, thinking that he might change his mind. I jumped off the couch, snatched the colourful packet off the shelf, tore it open, grabbed a yellow one, popped it straight in my mouth, and then repositioned myself on the couch to face the music. As I looked up at the white ceiling with its bright fluorescent light and chewing the sweet Jelly Babies, it took my mind off the horrible procedure taking place on the other part of my body, meaning my right arm.

My first blood test ever was a piece of cake or even a complete packet of Jelly Babies. I thought, at least I won't need another one.

But how wrong can one be?

As Dr Handley was dabbing my arm with cotton wool.

Probably mopping up my blood!

To my never-ending horror, he said,

"Right, that's it. You will need another blood test in six weeks. And next time, bring your own sweets. The sweets here are meant for the children, not for big soft adults."

Reluctantly, having no choice in the matter, I went back six weeks later and took my own sweets, Polo mints, by the way, because they had a much stronger taste and were better to suck on. Nowadays, I use chewing gum.

I was lying on the dreaded couch sucking away to my heart's content when everything regarding my precious blood withdrawal seemed to be going fine. Just like last time.

Amazingly, I felt quite relaxed.

Suddenly, with no warning, Dr Handley scared

the crap out of me.

He shouted,

"OH! NO! NO! NO!"

Absolutely terrified, I screamed,

"OH NO! WHAT'S UP?"

"Your blood is shooting out and squirting right up the wall."

"WHAT???"

With my shocked reaction, he burst out laughing.

I quickly realised it was only a joke and affectionately called him a swine and couldn't help but join in with his contagious laughter. But do you know? It worked. I had fun as I was having blood taken out of my traumatised body. Hey, what a great doctor.

After that amusing story, in other words, taking the pee out of me, or should I say blood, I will get back to the more essential things in life, such as cats, dogs and the occasional eccentric owner.

Cats

We never had cause to inject cats, that would have been a nightmare! But we did have to administer tablets. We did this by gently stroking their heads for a minute or two. Then we surprised them by gripping and pulling the loose skin at the back of their neck which gave a reflex action that made the mouth open. Then with no messing about, popping the tablet in with the other hand. To make sure that the tablet was swallowed we stroked the throat.

Job done.

Easy!

We were taught that trick by our vet.

Dogs

Often, dogs that needed injections had diabetes and required the horrible syringe once or twice daily. Now that is one disease I hope to avoid!

Besides injections, you would not believe the number of tablets and creams we used to administer. There were tablets for all sorts of ailments, and the containers and tubes came in all kinds of colours, shapes, and sizes. Of course, we had to make sure that the dogs had taken the correct tablets and, in some cases, we had to wrestle them down their throats. Talk about a pharmacy or even a vet's surgery. At times it looked like we could have had enough to supply the whole of the county.

Wrong Cat?

Busy collection days brought with them lots of chaos. We had to make sure that the cats and dogs were in tip-top condition. And everything they had brought in with them was going back home with them.

With cats being scrupulously clean animals, we did accept cat bedding, usually a jumper that probably had the scent of its owner on it.

There is one collection that I will always remember, or should I say a nightmare cat collection. The cat in question was a young kitten called Tabitha. She stayed with us for just over four weeks. Tabitha's owner's name was Mrs Riley. Tabitha was a typical tabby-coloured cat, hence the name Tabitha. She was growing rapidly, especially with her being only four months old.

The office was full of customers when Mrs Riley arrived to collect Tabitha.

After politely waiting her turn, she said,

"How is my lovely Tabitha? I cannot wait to see her."

With a smile, I replied,

"Oh, fine, she is gorgeous. You will be very lucky if the girls down at the cattery let you have her back."

After Mrs Riley paid her bill, I asked one of the girls,

"Jenny, can you fetch Tabitha, please?

Within ten minutes, Jenny arrived in the office with Tabitha safely installed in her carry container. By that time, the office was overflowing with customers. They were even queuing back onto the car park.

Mrs Riley bent down and peered through the container's white plastic mesh.

A puzzled look formed on her face.

To my embarrassment, she sternly pronounced in a concise voice, these dreaded words,

"THIS IS NOT MY CAT!"

It was just like dropping a bombshell.

The noisy office went dead quiet, and I mean dead, dead quiet.

I looked at her in amazement.

Embarrassed, I said,

"Yes, it is Mrs Riley."

She looked me straight in the eye.

She responded angrily,

"NO, IT IS NOT MR DOODY. THIS CAT IS NOT MY TABITHA. IT IS FAR TOO BIG!"

I looked straight back at her and defended myself,

"Yes, but while you have been away, she has grown. She has been here for more than four weeks and is still a kitten. Kittens grow very fast at her age."

She started to get angry with me and raised her voice even louder for all to hear on the car park,

"NO WAY! SHE COULD NOT POSSIBLY HAVE GROWN THAT BIG! THAT CAT IS DEFINITELY NOT MY LITTLE TABITHA! THIS CAT WHOEVER IT BELONGS TO IS ENORMOUS! IT IS NOT MY CAT. AND I DON'T WANT IT!

I winced, and with increasing embarrassment, furtively glanced around at the queue of customers. I could see that there was more than a lot of interest starting to show in our conversation or, should I say Mrs Riley's shouting match. Jenny, one of my best staff members who had taken care of Tabitha also tried to convince Mrs Riley that it was her cat.

But she was having none of it!

It was getting more like 'Fawlty Towers' by the second.

Forcing a smile as I tried to take control of the situation or to word it better, the entertaining farce.

I said,

"Mrs Riley, please come with me and Jenny down to the cattery. We will show you where Tabitha has stayed for the last four weeks. I will prove to you that she is your cat."

So, as the office full of customers looked on, I took Mrs Riley down to the cattery, (strangling her came to mind) as poor Kathy tried to convince the curious queue of customers that we were in the right and for sure Tabitha belonged to the angry Mrs Riley.

It is quite normal for kittens to grow rapidly, and because Mrs Riley had not seen her kitten for over four weeks, she would look a lot bigger than before. In fact, she had more than doubled in size.

Mrs Riley, who had gone very quiet, (probably seething) walked between Jenny and me down to the cattery. With Jenny backing me up, I showed her the cat run where her 'giant-sized cat' had been staying. Tabitha's name, delivery date and collection date were still attached to a card outside her door for all to see. Also, I took her around the full cattery as she scrutinised every door label and cat that was in residence. Finally, at long last, I convinced Mrs Riley that the star of the day's entertainment was waiting patiently in my office and that she was indeed her lovely

Tabitha.

Mrs Riley apologised and burst into shrieks of laughter in her realisation that her beloved miniature kitten, not exactly Godzilla, had doubled in size.

Back in the office to a round of applause, I joked with her and said,

"I'll cut Tabitha's food down the next time she stays here."

All I can say is it was a good job Mrs Riley hadn't been away for six months.

Wrong Dog?

Having just had the wrong cat; now it is the turn of the wrong dog, which is very different from Tabitha's story.

Once and only once, this wrong dog scenario happened, which makes this short story unique.

On another hectic day, a man who was doing a favour for his next-door neighbour came into the office, paid our bill and collected a Border Collie called Sam. Sam's true owner wasn't due back until later in the day and was worried that he might not make our closing time of 5 pm.

We found that Sam was by far the most popular name for dogs and, for some reason, especially Border Collies.

And that, my friends, is the only excuse I can offer for what happens next...

Just over three hours after Sam the Border Collie had left our premises, I received a phone call from his distressed owner who had just arrived home from his holiday.

He said,

"This is not my Sam. It says Sam on his collar, but I can assure you this is not my Sam. There is a disc attached to this dog's collar that says, Sam Jones. I am Mr Phillips."

Fictitious names, by the way, to avoid any embarrassment. Especially for me!

'OH NO! Who's going to get a rollicking this time?'

For sure, guaranteed it would be me.

To my relief, Mr Phillips said,

"Shall I bring him back?"

In my jesting mind, I thought,

'That would be quite a good idea.'

I bit my tongue and politely said,

"Oh, yes, please. I am terribly sorry. I cannot believe we made such a stupid mistake."

Several hours after leaving our premises, Sam Jones came back from his adventure and temporary home. He wagged his tail furiously and was swapped for the rightful Sam Phillips, with no damage done. Thank goodness we were in a lull, and no other customers were around to see just how proficient we were not.

Mr Phillips took the correct Sam away and thankfully saw the funny side of the story as he left with a smile on his face. It is probably no surprise to anyone reading this story that we omitted to tell Mr Jones about his Sam's surprise excursion to a new home. Who knows what his reaction would have been? Unlike Mr Philips, he may not have seen the funny side of things. And I have to say. It was a good job Sam Jones couldn't talk.

Fashion And Greetings

Sometimes I found it quite amazing how customers dressed, especially the ladies when they collected their pets. Especially when they collected dogs!

One miserable wet day, we had a lady who arrived in the pouring rain. She wasn't dressed as you would expect in waterproof clothing, but clothes that I am sure she would have felt much more comfortable wearing in a posh restaurant. The attractive lady was wearing a pink top and a tight white skirt. She had come to collect my mate Ben, the large, boisterous golden Labrador who starred in the second chapter. She was waiting in anticipation as she crouched down by the outside door of kennel block one waiting for Ben to trot out and gently lick her hand.

But Ben never came out quite as calmly as that. Did he?

No, Ben just launched himself straight at her, like a heat-seeking missile. He immediately placed his front paws on his mistress's shoulders, knocking her down onto the ground. She never got a chance to stand up to greet him before the over-excited Ben covered the expensive-looking pink top and white skirt with big wet paw marks. But can you believe it? She didn't seem to mind.

The other amazing thing we witnessed was how some owners let their dogs greet them. They bent down and let them lick around their faces and mouths. And as they smiled, can you believe it? Their dogs sometimes licked their teeth. Worms??? Yuk, yuk!

There is a disgusting story about a dog called Stubby. For sure, you would not want to get anywhere near his tongue! I will tell you his story in a later book.

I would like to have asked some dog owners this question,

"Have you ever heard of dogs eating faeces or having worms?"

But of course, I never did.

This next story is about a lovely lady getting into a predicament when we had an office full of customers.

A feminine voice called from the back of the queue,

"Can you please help me, Mr Doody?"

Everybody turned around to see an attractive blonde standing at the back of the queue. She was wearing shiny tight black leather trousers with a light pink designer low-cut top. The bad news was...

It was covered in vomit!

The vomit had been manufactured and deposited by her cat. The cat had been sitting on her lap as she was driving to our premises. The vomit had pebble-dashed her lovely clothing, and none of the male admirers in the office was in a big hurry to volunteer to wipe it off. I must admit with me being used to vomit, pee and lots of crap, I was quite tempted to help, but I thought my neck would stay unbroken if I let Kathy do it instead.

I could never understand why some customers didn't think to put a towel on their laps to protect their clothing.

Some cats arrived on customer's laps instead

of in their carriers because many cats did not like being in them and most certainly hated travelling in them. The owners took the risk that their cat could vomit, pee, or even do the unthinkable, crap on their laps instead of in their carriers. Maybe the cats preferred travelling this way, so they could teach their owners a lesson or two for leaving them behind for a couple of weeks. Cats can be very crafty like that.

I have witnessed such happenings on many occasions. I know it's no joke when a pet travels in a vehicle and is ill during the journey. On many occasions, I have had first-hand experience with this problem.

But…

I most certainly made sure it wasn't on my lap. That is another amusing story for the future.

And for sure, the police would not be too impressed with the way some pets travelled to our premises.

The Telephone

The other thing we had to contend with on busy days was numerous phone calls that needed answering immediately because we never wanted to miss the chance of a booking. Not only would the office be overflowing with customers, cats and dogs coming and going, but often we would be inundated with very lengthy phone calls. Most of the calls were for new bookings, but the ones that amazed me were from sensitive owners who had just dropped off their cat or dog only half an hour before. They just needed to know if their babies were missing them and had settled in during their stay at 'Alcatraz'. Well, they didn't say 'Alcatraz', but I am sure you know what I mean. How could we possibly tell if their cat or dog was missing them after only half an hour had passed?

I couldn't say,

"Cancel your holiday, or your pet will never forgive you."

Everything had to be perfect. That is why we were there.

We even had customers who wanted to talk to their dog or cat over the phone, and quite a few phoned from abroad.

Here is an example,

"Is it possible to get *'Rover'* or *'Tiddles'* to the telephone? He can recognise my voice."

'I cannot believe I am hearing this. Are you kidding me, or what?'

Anyway, I solved that little problem. It was remarkable how adept I had become at meowing and barking down the phone. It was a little bit embarrassing when you did it in front of an office full of customers though.

Hey, I'm only joking!

One of those days when we were relatively steady rather than busy, we had a postcard from one dog owner who was holidaying in Florida. The dog's name was Bruno. He was a Doberman and quite friendly toward people but a bully, especially where small dogs were concerned.

I have a future story about Bruno and a St Bernard named Lady and how she taught him a lesson he would never forget.

Adverts for my next book just keep on coming!

When I sent for Bruno, we had three customers in the office. I told them that his owner had sent a postcard and wished me to read it to Bruno. So, in front of the disbelieving witnesses, I proceeded to read out the postcard contents to the intelligent Doberman. He cocked his ears in my direction and appeared to listen to every word. When I had finished reading, and Bruno had played his part, he was led out of the office wagging his stubby tail.

A man who witnessed the event said,

"I've just about seen everything now."

I don't know if the customers who had witnessed our act thought I had gone stark-staring bonkers or if it was just another one of Geoff's PR stunts. Maybe I was just taking the Mickey. Well, at least I knew I wasn't stark, staring bonkers, and so did Bruno.

Pre-Release

This event always seemed to happen on one of those mega, mega-busy days.

A guy turned up in a red hatchback car, and as I watched through my office window, he appeared to read one of our signs right in front of his car.

The sign read:

PLEASE KEEP YOUR DOGS IN THE CAR UNTIL YOUR DOCUMENTS HAVE BEEN CHECKED

Totally ignoring what he had read, with no hesitation, he lifted the tailgate, and four dogs of all shapes and sizes exploded out like shrapnel in four different directions to various parts of the planet. Or should I say our premises. Within seconds and to my annoyance, they found four of my beautiful shrubs to cock their legs up. The foursome's owner bawled out all their names as he gave chase, but it was fruitless. They ran rings around him. Were they disobedient, or what?

Have you ever noticed that dogs, when they are

somewhere new and having fun, often seem to ignore their frustrated owner's commands? For sure, it always seems to fall on deaf ears.

The foursome created absolute mayhem. They ran up to and sniffed several of our customers who were standing patiently on the car park, with their dogs fastened securely on leads. They had already had their dog's veterinary passports checked and were waiting for a staff member to take their dog for its introductory walk.

Eventually, one of the four dogs came back to their owner, who by now had become very, very angry. So, what did he do next? He gave the unfortunate dog a clip around its ear. Now, in the canine mind, why on earth would you want to go back to your owner if you are going to get a clip around the ear? Especially when you have just obeyed his or her instructions. It would be much more sensible and rewarding for a dog to receive a gentle stroke on the head and maybe a biscuit or two and be told what a good dog you are for coming back even though it had not been immediate. It is quite normal for dogs to have a good run around when given their newfound freedom, and you can't blame them for getting excited when they unexpectedly find they are in unexplored territory.

By his body language and loud voice, the foursome's owner was very frustrated and had no success with the other three. He was sweating profusely, obviously in the most seething of tempers. His small pack would not come back to his continuous shouting. I wonder why?

So, it was up to our busy staff to give up their valuable time and leave what they were doing to help this certain gentleman to catch his dogs as they continued to run riot.

Eventually, all the dogs were caught with no help from their owner. Perhaps the next time, he would read my sign and wouldn't get himself into such an embarrassing situation, especially in front of all the other sensible dog owners who watched on. I must say the customers waiting at that time appeared to be enjoying the spectacle he and his dogs had provided. Thank goodness his dogs or other dogs waiting on the car park were not aggressive to each other.

Once the hapless owner had left, we took his four excited dogs for a walk around the woodland to calm them down. During their stay and a little training from me, they were much more obedient than when they arrived.

Decision Time?

On a few occasions, ladies and even some men left our office crying their eyes out because they were leaving their loved ones behind. And I do not mean their husband or wife. Other customers seeing them shedding tears could be quite shocked, imagining that maybe their pet had just died in our care. I soon put that one right and explained why they were crying. Yet again, the last thing we wanted was false rumours of hordes of pets dying on our premises.

We could virtually guarantee that a potential customer would turn up out of the blue to view our facilities on busy days. It was very time-consuming, but we had to be patient because they were our future. Occasionally, we had the laid-back one who could see our staff running around like headless chickens but still took all the time in the world. We didn't mind at all when we weren't busy, but when they just turned up without an appointment and the office was full of customers, it made life just a little bit awkward, to say the least. Sometimes we had more patience than a Saint, but it gave us great satisfaction when they eventually made a booking.

Some customers were quite considerate when they could see that we were run off our feet and volunteered to complete the booking forms in their cars. The frustrating thing was when some pet owners could not make up their minds and dithered,

"Should I, or shouldn't I?"

Well, they would hum and ha, and if they were a couple, they often passed the responsibility back and forth before making the final decision. It didn't seem to matter one iota to the potential customer that they were delaying a queue of other customers who had made appointments with us.

Long-standing customers often came to our rescue because no matter what information we gave the potential customer, it didn't seem to make them hurry up. Our regular customers did not shout out,

"Get a move on, will you? And make up your minds. We need to be attended to as well; we have a plane to catch!"

No, they politely recommend to potential customers how often they had brought their dog or cat to us and how happy their pet had always been when they had eventually collected them. Usually, that did the trick. So, the potential customer usually booked on the spot and was out of the office far quicker than me trying to convince them.

But as usual, there is always one.

The lady in question was Mrs Oaks, she owned a Rottweiler bitch called Meg. As I have mentioned before, Rottweilers do have a dubious reputation, but Meg turned out to be gorgeous, or should I say 'as soft as a brush'. Mrs Oaks was a middle-aged widow, and she appeared to be quite wealthy. She told me that she had for-gone many exotic holidays over the three years she had owned Meg. The numerous customers in the office and myself were getting a full life history of how she looked after Meg in-between her busy work schedule. Also, how much she desperately wanted to go to the Bahamas with a group of friends for three weeks. She informed me that she had inspected quite a few kennels in the area over the last three years. The good news was, she thought our kennels were excellent, and they were by far the best she had ever seen.

I am blowing my trumpet again!

Eventually, numerous customers who were collecting and delivering, convinced Mrs Oaks that she would have absolutely nothing to worry about, assuring her that Meg would enjoy her stay with us. They, with added enthusiasm, advised her how often we walked the dogs, brushed, bathed, and played with them. Also, how contented their own dog had been when it stayed with us. And very often, the dog did not want to go back home.

I promised Mrs Oaks that I would personally walk and look after Meg myself. At least it helped to persuade her to leave the busy office. Boy, it took some patience, but it was those helpful customers that mainly achieved it with only a little help from me. So, at long last, Mrs Oaks finally booked.

Wow, that was a hard one to convince!

I adhered to my promise like super glue. I have always been a man of my word, and thank goodness I was because I would never have been fortunate to have met the lovely Meg. She was a pleasure to be with, and I got quite attached to her. It reminded me of the early days when I looked after the cats and dogs on my own and made quite a lot of new furry friends.

In the latter years with the business being so busy, having an abundance of willing staff, the maintenance of the grounds to take care of and three Springer Spaniels of my own, it was a very rare occurrence that I helped with dog walking. But in Meg's case, I made an exception. And what a wonderful decision it was!

The three weeks with Meg went very quickly, and it soon came to the time when I would sadly have to hand Meg back to her fretting owner, who, by the way, had phoned every single day from the Bahamas, checking how the lovely Meg was coping with Alcatraz.

When Mrs Oaks finally arrived to collect Meg, she was a very distressed lady, almost a nervous wreck. She fired endless questions at me. I couldn't answer her fast enough before she hit me with the next one. Eventually, I calmed her down and sorted out the paperwork, which was quite a large bill.

I entered the kennel block, ensuring that I left the outside security door open. I walked down the row of runs to Meg's kennel and opened the mesh gate to her run. Without putting her on the lead, I ran with Meg right on my heels straight out of the building. We ran out onto the car park where Mrs Oaks was eagerly waiting. Then the unbelievable happened...

Well, it was for Mrs Oaks. Meg just had a quick sniff of her owner's ankles, briefly wagged her stumpy docked tail and came bounding right back over to me and sat at my side, pressing herself up against my legs almost pushing me over.

I will never forget that look of amazement on Mrs Oaks's face as I said,

"Does that tell you anything?"

She was astonished by Meg's unexpected behaviour and said,

"I can't believe it. I'm astounded. It tells me what a fool I've been over the last three years. I've worried about Meg every day of my holiday. Well, at least I know I can book as many holidays as I like. And I will never have to worry about my Meg again because she will be boarding here."

That was one happy dog and owner and for me, complete job satisfaction. Also, I was delighted because not only would I see Meg again many times in the coming years, it would be very good for our reputation.

So, in those following years, as promised, I always made sure I found time to take care of my lovely Meg.

CHAPTER 9

Ken's Terrifying Ordeal

This is a very, very funny story about Kathy's brother Ken, but it starts off with two friends who have volunteered to help with the dog walking.

As I have mentioned previously, to keep costs down, it was necessary to refrain from employing staff for as long as possible. In those days with us being tied to the business we held many dinner parties at our cottage. We found it was better to stay on the premises to ensure we were caring one hundred per cent after our furry guests.

Two long-standing friends Rick and Bet, (depicted in the caricature) often came to our cottage for dinner. Rick was my best man at our wedding a few years before. He was a retired very successful businessman and always dressed very smartly. Rick phoned me with a wonderful idea. He suggested that he and Bet would like to come a little earlier before dinner and help us to walk the dogs.

'What a great idea, any free help we will never refuse.'

Thoughtfully, Bet brought a change of clothing because she envisaged walking excited dogs around the woodland, resulting in muddy paws soiling her clothes. For some reason, known only to Rick, he chose to walk the dogs wearing a smart jacket and tie. For sure, it was not the correct attire for dog walking, but I have to say Rick was the best-dressed dog walker of all time. We even have that walking session on video.

Rick and Bet had great fun and helped us on numerous occasions during our first summer. It was quite a novelty to them, and it added great stories around the dining table. It started a trend with many of our friends and, of course, not forgetting our family members.

In other words, if they didn't help us walk the dogs...

They got no dinner!

It doesn't matter how often I review this next story. I cannot help but imagine what is going on in this certain person's head. It makes me laugh out loud every time I read it, and I am sure it will do the same for you.

So, here comes Ken.

Kathy's brother Ken and his wife Rosemarie are both from farming backgrounds. I would describe my brother-in-law as a typical farmer's son, with rosy cheeks and a cheeky smile. He is well-weathered, as strong as an ox and just over six feet tall. He could drive a combine harvester, a massive four-wheel-drive tractor, wield an axe, or use a chainsaw, probably all in the same day. He wouldn't have looked out of place as a doorman, wearing a DJ and bow tie standing outside the front entrance to a posh nightclub. He gave the impression he wouldn't be afraid of anything or anybody.

So, what on earth could possibly frighten big strong Ken?

Well, that answer is coming!

It was a lovely Sunday evening when Ken and Rosemarie set about their new task of dog walking. They teamed up with Kathy and Ann. On that evening I did not walk the dogs. Instead, I stayed in the kennels and organised which dogs each walker should take.

Boarding with us was a very old black Labrador called Bess. She had a lovely nature and wouldn't hurt a fly. As she approached you wagging her tail, she had a disconcerting habit of curling her upper lip back. I called it a happy grin. I have noticed quite a lot of Labradors do this.

Take note.

Anyone knowing not too much about dogs, especially when dogs curl their lips back, could easily mistake this greeting, as a nasty, aggressive, vicious, silent snarl.

And big strapping Ken, our intrepid new dogwalker, knew very little about dogs!

Unfortunately for Bess, she had arthritis and had suffered a stroke six months before. It had caused her to hold her head on one side, and her eyes seemed to show only the whites. I must say, she did look rather peculiar or even creepy. As you can imagine, poor old Bess was on her last legs, albeit very happy enjoying what little life she had left. I had warned Bess's owners that she may not last the duration. I explained that the kennels were a very different environment compared to her home. And every day for Bess would be a bonus. I pointed out that she could expire at any moment. Her caring owners accepted the risks involved. So, we agreed to board Bess for the duration of their much-needed two-week holiday.

I installed old Bess just inside the kennel block in the first run closest to the exit door. I did this because it was adjacent to the car park and the large lawn that ran down to the cattery and our cottage. This enabled us to let her out on her own where she was free to take care of herself. Sadly, in her condition, she wasn't going far. It was impossible to walk her around the wood because she was just not fit enough. Bess was an exceptionally clean dog and always waited for us to let her out. As soon as she had walked, or even stumbled ten yards, once her feet touched the grass, she instantly squatted down to relieve herself. Within minutes one of us would check on her and scoop up the result. When she had finished her business, she was quite happy to stagger about having a few sniffs here and there before slowly making her way back to her run. Bess had been doing this for almost two weeks and had gotten into her happy routine. We trusted her and left her to her own devices.

Take note.

Big fearless Ken knew absolutely nothing at all about Bess and her harmless roaming routine.

And I never thought to enlighten him!

Ken returned from the woodland walk with two well-behaved yellow Labradors. I planned to pass him two more dogs on leads for his next trip around the wood. This was the easiest and quickest method for dog walking sessions when we had help. Although every run's mesh gate was labelled, I knew off by heart which one each dog belonged to. Ken with a big smile on his face was obviously enjoying himself. He started to walk along the long row of runs with his two new-found friends. He was just about to hand the two Labs over to me.

And this is when the fun started!

I couldn't help but notice, Ken's smile had faded.

He was preoccupied with something behind me.

His eyes reflected a look of sheer terror.

His jaw had dropped open, and he had gone as white as a sheet.

'What on earth is he staring at?'

I turned around to look and see what had taken his undivided attention.

I couldn't help but smile, because low and behold, there was poor old Bess.

She staggered drunkenly past her run towards Ken and me.

Her head lolled to one side.

Her curled upper lip revealed menacing yellow crooked teeth.

Only the whites of her eyes were showing.

Her tail slowly wagged from side to side.

This was too much for Ken to comprehend.

He took one look at her and shouted,

"OH NO!"

I turned around, and to my amazement, Ken had gone.

Ken had vacated the kennels at a blinding speed.

The two bewildered Labradors had no choice...

They were going as well!

Ken was going so fast his legs were a blur.

The Labs were falling over each other in a bid to keep up.

Ken didn't care!

With six feet of solid muscle, Ken was running away from poor old Bess.

Off he shot back into the wood.

The Labs must have thought it was their lucky day. After a nice leisurely walk, they were now going out for another that could only be described as a gallop.

When I looked into Ken's eyes, I could only imagine what was going on inside his head and how terrified he was of poor old black Bess. I started to laugh, and I couldn't stop. I had tears streaming down my cheeks, and all the dogs were looking at me as if I had gone mad.

Finally, after a few minutes, I managed to pull

myself together.

Kathy appeared in the kennels leading a pair of Dalmatians.

She gave me a puzzled look and said,

"Why is Ken running around the wood with those Labs again?"

I gave her one look and my laughter erupted again, and so did the tears. I was laughing so much I couldn't answer.

Kathy had a puzzled look on her face.

She said,

"What have you done to my brother this time?"

Well, I had played a few harmless pranks on Ken in the past, and Kathy thought that I might have been up to something again.

Trying to control my laughter, I said,

"Honestly, Kathy, I haven't done anything. Your Ken is frightened to death of poor old Bess."

Again, I went into fits of laughter.

What do you mean, he is frightened of old Bess?

I struggled through my laughter to explain to Kathy just how it had come to pass why her big hunk of a brother had taken flight from an old crippled dog.

Finally, she got the gist of the situation and erupted into bursts of laughter. Ann and Rosemarie arrived back in the kennels with their charges. On hearing about Ken's hilarious dilemma, they joined in as well. Ken's rapid departure created a chorus of laughter that echoed all around the kennels. The four of us laughed hysterically and almost had to hold each other up. The dogs in the kennels joined in the chorus with their barking and yapping. They must have thought we had gone stark-staring bonkers.

Eventually, we calmed down.

Then we heard Ken's stern voice shouting from the wood,

“WILL SOMEBODY COME AND TAKE THESE

DOGS OFF ME?"

We all burst out laughing again.

I went into the wood to rescue him, trying hard to restrain my laughter.

Ken was not amused!

He said,

"What the are you doing, letting killer dogs roam loose in your kennels?"

I burst out laughing again, and I could hear the three girls echoing my laughter back in the kennels.

"What's so funny, anyway? What are you all laughing at?"

"If you come back into the kennels, I'll show you exactly what's so funny."

"You'll never get me back in those kennels again!"

Anyway, Ken was proven wrong, because, with a bit of coaxing and trying to keep our faces straight, we eventually got him back into the kennel block.

Well, Kathy did.

He certainly didn't trust me!

After explaining poor old Bess's condition, Kathy led Ken like a placid lamb to formally introduce him to the illusion that had frightened the life out of him. By then Bess was safely back in her run. Cautiously, Ken stood outside her run. She gave Ken that same old grin, curling her upper lip as she wagged her tail from side to side. He looked down at poor old Bess, and I noticed his facial expression. I still wasn't sure if he was entirely convinced that she wasn't a rabid dog.

Later that evening over dinner, Ken told me he thought Bess looked like the Devil's dog, as she had staggered, lurched, and lumbered towards him. To Ken's credit, it never stopped him from helping us in the future, and we never had another dog like Bess that we needed to warn him about.

Even after all these years, Ken still doesn't see the funny side of this story, and I am sure he thinks I set him up on purpose.

It is so amusing. I only wish I had!

CHAPTER 10

Teeth Versus Claws?

Well, we have had some fun with dogs, and now it is the turn of our feline friends...Cats.

It may come as a complete surprise to you, but in my opinion, cats are far more dangerous than dogs. When you think about it, it is quite logical because cats have five sets of weaponry, starting with their teeth backed up by four sharp hooked claws on each foot.

Dogs only have one weapon, their teeth. Having stated that I have met quite a few dogs that remind me of the great white shark in the film Jaws, but unlike sharks with most dogs, you usually get some kind of warning. In my vast experience, very often you do not get any warning at all with a dangerous cat.

One thing that all cats love to do is sharpen their claws, whether it is on a tree, scratching post, or even your expensive furniture. Have you ever been to someone's house where their cat has clawed the furniture? What a mess they make with their lethal claws. The other major weapon in a cat's armoury is a very nasty set of sharp needle-like teeth that lurk in a small, very powerful jaw.

Cat's teeth are far more dangerous than dogs because they can penetrate the skin more easily, especially if it is of a delicate human variety such as mine. Also, cats carry bacteria due to their varied diet of live animals and birds, leaving leftover flesh rotting between their teeth. Unlike humans, no dental floss or toothpicks for them!

So, if anyone or anything is bitten by a cat, the risk of infection is very high. You could say that a cat's bite is a little like a venomous snake with the added danger of four sets of claws that move like lightning. So, in other words, cats can be a very dangerous adversary indeed. We had many cats boarding with us, that were recovering from abscesses. The horrible abscesses seeping with puss will have been inflicted during a catfight. Probably with a neighbour's cat.

I can honestly say that I love cats, but I am more frightened, or should I say wary of a cat compared to a dog, especially when it is in full attack mode. I became aware that the percentage of cats becoming dangerous was probably twenty-five per cent higher than dogs. And that was far too high for my liking.

After many years of running the pet hotel, we only experienced a few cats that were difficult to deal with. The majority of our boarders were placid and loved to be fussed.

On a cat's departure day, the problem with some of the aggressive little blighters was we needed to pick them up and install them in their carry containers.

I often thought,

'*Why not send the cat's owner down to the cattery to put the love of their life back into their carriers?*'

Now, that was an excellent idea, but some owners wouldn't even pick their cats up. No way would they go down to the cattery and help.

Sometimes I would like to have said,

"If you won't, or you can't pick up your cat, then how are we expected to do it?"

I am sure their reply would have been,

"Well, you are the experts."

And of course we were.

But sometimes for sure, we wished we weren't, but it was the job that we had chosen. So, we had no choice but to get on with it and face the music. Did I say music? The way some of those cats yowled, boy, it was a long way from the sound of music.

Although we were pretty-much experts, I have to admit that we didn't always quite know how to deal with the occasional vicious little tiger guesting in the cattery. When we had trouble with a cat that would not go into its carrier, who do you think had to do the dirty work? Yes, you guessed it, send for good old Geoff. When summoned, I charged down to the cattery like a knight in shining armour, but unfortunately, without any armour. Believe me, I needed armour at times, although I did wear a strong pair of gloves with long cuffs that I had purchased from our vets. Can you imagine what trouble vets must have with some of the felines brought to their surgeries? Well, at least they could sedate them.

I learnt from a vet that the most efficient way of picking up a cat is by the loose skin at the base of the neck. When some people witness this method, they think it looks cruel, but it doesn't hurt them one little bit. Also, this is how their mothers used to carry them when they were kittens.

Grabbing the scruff of a cat's neck was sometimes a problem because the front end is protected by fangs and teeth. And not forgetting the four razor-sharp claws, especially the formidable ones at the back. So that was why I needed to be much craftier than the far-from-placid cat awaiting my attention.

My method was to wave a towel in my left hand that would hopefully distract my intelligent opponent from the action of my gloved right hand. Then slowly I would try to manoeuvre the cat into the corner of its run, trying hard not to frighten it. Then with my gloved right hand, swiftly grab it by the scruff of its neck. (A bit like a snake catcher with a king cobra.) As I did this, I dropped the towel leaving my left hand free. This enabled me to grab the base of the cat's tail. Then I was able to lift the cat, which brought more weapons into play, meaning the four sets of claws, especially the ones at the back. Not forgetting the bad-tempered yowling! By now, you should be getting the picture.

If a cat did manage to make contact with anything human, meaning one of my staff or me, or if it could hook its claws around something else, no way would it let go. We just had to do our best to prise the cat off whatever it had attached itself to. And believe me, it was not easy. A crowbar did come to mind!

The moment I suspended my feline friend a few inches from the floor the spitting and growling would erupt, and it would scream blue murder. This is where I needed help from another staff member with the cat carrier at hand. I can assure you that it took quite some skill and bravery from the two of us to get that little bundle of spitting fighting fury gently lowered with precision into its carrier. From start to finish, the process had to be done within seconds because if it wasn't, it meant that you had failed and lost the battle. And if that was the case, other methods had to be used, which I will come to later. Fortunately, in most cases, my gloved-hand approach usually worked, and with all the practice we became quite skilful.

The girls from the cattery knew which cats were likely to cause problems because they would have grown to know their little habits during their stay. Like trying to rip them to bits! Thankfully, a good percentage of the cats walked into their carrier. Others just needed a little bit of friendly persuasion. I have had quite a few small cats frighten the hell out of me. They say the worst big cats in the world for bad tempers are leopards. And I can tell you I have met a few little leopards in our cattery a few times. The owners wanted their little leopards at home as quickly as possible, and I can assure you, so did we. The day before yesterday would not have been soon enough.

Some cats only turned nasty because they hated their cat carriers. One moment a cat could be friendly and lovable, but once it saw its carrier, it probably thought something unpleasant was about to happen. It probably had connections in the cat's memory of a trip down to the vet's surgery for a painful injection or even something nastier such as castration. So, we couldn't blame our feline friends for associating the cat carrier with unpleasant experiences, usually meaning pain.

If all else failed to get the spitting growling bundle of fur into its carrier, then more extreme measures were necessary, and that is when we used one of Geoff's new toys.

The dreaded cat tongs!

The cat tongs were an implement or even a defensive weapon that I had purchased from our local vets. The instructions on the box read, 'Only use in extreme emergencies'. One emergency was one too many for my liking. Cat tongs are like fireplace tongs used to place coal onto a fire or rearrange the hot coals within. Yes, we could be dealing with a red-hot cat rather than red-hot coals.

Was there a difference? I ask myself.

The cat tongs were about two feet long and designed to clamp around the cat's neck, which enabled the user, meaning the more than cautious little me, to pin the cat down safely. Then I could hopefully grab it by the scruff of the neck. I know it sounds a bit brutal, but we had no choices in some cases. You will soon realise this when you read my next story.

Mr Tiddles

Once upon a time, (I always wanted to write that) a cat called Mr Tiddles was leaving the cattery after a two-week stay. According to the cattery girls Pat and Jenny, he had been a perfect, well-behaved cuddly guest. But his mood was about to change big time because as soon as he saw his cat carrier, he was not the nice Mr Tiddles we knew minutes before. To the girls surprise, the cat from hell replaced him. A furious bad-tempered angry leopard had taken his place. And when I say angry, I mean angry!

Did I mention blood?

So, here comes the armoured gloved routine.

Speaking to Mr Tiddles in my soft coaxing voice, I waved my unprotected left hand in front of his nose, therefore keeping his attention well away from my sneaky right gloved hand. In other words, that was the hand that was going to do the business. So, before he realised what the heck was going on, my gloved right hand pounced and successfully grabbed him by the scruff of his neck...

And that is when all hell broke loose!

Accompanied by a loud growl, or should I say shriek, Mr Tiddles legs shot out sideways. With his claws extended he attached himself to the four sides of his carrier. He was growling and spitting as I struggled to hold him. Pat and Jenny were doing their utmost best to bend his rigid legs into his carrier. For sure, there was absolutely no way the little demon was ever going in his carrier. And no way was the little terror going to give in.

Mr Tiddles owners Mr & Mrs Browning had been patiently waiting in my office. After our unsuccessful titanic struggle with the cat from hell, we suggested maybe they should go down to the cattery and try to get the little monster in the cat carrier themselves. To give them credit, they agreed to have a go which I thought was very sporting of them, especially with them being aware of his hatred for the carrier. The brave couple tried various ways to bag him up, so to speak. I watched them doing battle and kept well out of the way of the contest that was taking place.

But, the furiously angry Mr Tiddles was having none of it!

The more they tried, the more ferocious Mr Tiddles got. His fur was completely puffed out, and his ears flattened to his head, with yellow teeth bared. He was supposed to be a pet tabby cat, but he looked more like a Scottish Highland Wildcat by the second, and I can assure you, you don't mess about with them.

Mrs Browning looked at me in despair and said,

"I have never seen him act like this before. I know he doesn't like his carrier, but this is ridiculous. What on earth are we going to do?"

I had an idea,

'Fetch the shotgun!'

So, I had no alternative but to introduce my brand-new toy, the dreaded cat tongs.

With the cat tongs in my right-hand dangling down the side of my leg, hoping that Mr Tiddles hadn't noticed, I locked myself inside his run. He was huddled up in the corner, looking exhausted and terrified after his traumatic struggle. I must admit, I was beginning to feel sorry for him.

Anyway, that soon changed!

As soon as Mr Tiddles saw Geoff's magic tongues, the little devil had another lease of life. His adrenaline started to flow, and he became even more aggressive than ever. The yowling noise he made was way, way worse in comparison to the stunt that he had pulled earlier with the armoured glove scenario. I would never have believed a little cat could make as much noise as he yowled and snarled. And to add to my dismay, I could not fail to notice his sharp yellow teeth protruding out of his bright red gums. It was quite apparent that this cat had seen tongs before. Probably at the vets. And, I was getting a distinct impression he didn't like them one little bit. So, the magic tongs weren't so magic after all because Mr Tiddles went absolutely berserk. He was going absolutely ballistic, and I was the one locked in a run with a bad-tempered leopard cat.

As I moved forward, holding the cat tongs, he started to ricochet off the walls, uncomfortably close to my face, and even worse, my eyes. And he was screaming blue murder.

As well as the intrepid owners, quite a large audience meaning most of my staff had gathered to watch the entertainment. I am sure they were waiting to see whose blood was to be spilt first.

Mr Tiddles or mine!

Guess what? Everyone thought it was going to be mine.

During the struggle, another staff member came to the cattery to inform us that two new customers had turned up and wanted to view the cattery.

'Oh no, that's the last thing we need.'

I looked at Pat who was mesmerised by the epic battle between cat and human.

My mind raced, and I said,

"Quick Pat! Go back up to the office, and whatever you do, do not let them come anywhere near the cattery. Please wait until we come back up to the office. I hate to think what they will think with all this noise going on. It sounds more like we are killing cats, not taking care of them. Please show them some nice dogs or something. Do anything. Just keep them well away from here. Go! Go! Go!"

In my clear-cut message to Pat, I felt like swearing, which was not my usual practice and certainly not in front of customers, but I think whatever I uttered, Mr and Mrs Browning would have understood. The good news was, it was raining quite hard so Pat should not have too much of a problem keeping the prospective customers entertained in the office. But I was getting more and more frustrated with Mr Tiddles, and I am sure he wanted to kill me in his temper. I was doing my best to keep as calm as possible, and it didn't help the situation, especially with his owners watching.

Eventually, the exhausted Mr Tiddles succumbed to the cat tongs, and we safely installed him in his carrier. Mr and Mrs Browning thought I was very brave. Hey, and so did I! They sympathised with me and apologised profusely for their little pussycat's misdemeanour. Brave, I was for sure because there was blood on the floor tiles, and it was all mine, not one drop from our little leopard impressionist.

During one of his spectacular flights, which would have put a jet fighter to shame, Mr Tiddles had nicked my right ear lobe as he flew past with his claws extended. And I always insisted I would never get my ears pierced! After that little episode, I was certainly not into body piercing, especially after discovering just how painful it could be. When I finally nailed the ill-tempered little devil and closed the lid on his carrier, a naughty private thought crossed my mind.

'I should nail it down for good!'

When we walked back to the office with the back-to-normal placid little Mr Tiddles, I couldn't believe that the cheeky little devil was purring away as if nothing had happened.

On hearing him, Mrs Browning looked at me sheepishly and said,

"Would you have Mr Tiddles again?"

'That's got to be the question of the year.'

Putting that naughty thought away, I said,

"Of course, we will, but next time, please bring some tranquilisers with you. You will be able to get them from your vets. We will give them to him a couple of hours before you come to collect him."

At that moment, I wasn't sure who needed the tranquilisers, Mr Tiddles or me!

Ben With A Capital B

My mother's cat Ben was high up on the dangerous category list. He was possibly the number-one contender. He was yet another Jekyll and Hyde, and there were lots of them about, especially where cats were concerned. Ben used to stay in the cattery quite often, especially in the wintertime when we had our holidays which was the low season in our trade.

Irene, my mother, used to stay in our cottage to take care of things and answer the phone when the girls were busy. As I mentioned previously, we had an answering machine, but I preferred to use my mother's false posh voice instead. Hence, Ben used to stay in the cattery free of charge. You can't charge your mother, especially when she's doing you one heck of a favour. Can you? (Mind you, I do know certain people that would). But the conniving Ben should have been charged double!

There was no need to fill in the cat-booking form to find out Ben's temperament because we all knew what he was like. In fact, on the cat-booking form we didn't have, what is your cat's temperament? Generally, it was never necessary to know, although it might have been a good idea in some cases.

On Ben's numerous visits to the cattery, he turned out to be a real con artist. All the girls were informed of his violent nature and warned not to be fooled by him. But I think he got all of them at least once because they couldn't resist his initial charms. The number of rubber gloves he ruined with his lightning-extended claws doesn't bear thinking about.

Ben did not look like a wild-minded cat at all. In fact, just the opposite. He looked quite cute and cuddly and as innocent as a teddy bear. His colouring was predominantly grey on top, with white running down under his chin, chest, and stomach. We found with cats, their cuddly appearances can be quite deceptive, and Ben certainly looked cuddly.

Kathy had obtained Ben as a six-week-old kitten from a friend who had a farm in Cheshire. Mother was ill in bed with a bout of flu; Kathy thought it would cheer her up to have a tiny playful kitten to keep her company. Initially, Ben certainly worked wonders because he spent most of his time on her bed. When mother's bout of flu cleared, he would lie on her knee where he loved to stretch out upside-down with his legs in the air and get tickled on his tummy. Yes, Ben was a lovely playful kitten.

But as he grew, he changed... BIG TIME!

When visiting my mother's house, you would be sitting quite comfortably on the sofa, minding your own business. Ben would come up to you purring loudly. His tail would be swishing high in the air. It was obvious he wanted a fuss made of him. He would lovingly press and rub his head up and down your legs, just as most of the small feline tribe do. Well, let's face it, that's why we keep the little characters as pets. Isn't it?

Ben was no exception to the rule, but the difference with him was it was just one of his many ploys. For sure, he would lead you into a false sense of security. You could be holding your cup of tea in one hand as you tickled and stroked him with the other. Purring away, he appeared to enjoy the loving attention and would press his body even harder against your hand, just as if he was asking for more attention. Or was he? Suddenly, with no warning at all, he would hiss and spit as he took a swipe at your hand or any other body part that was in the range of his lightning-razor-sharp claws. Ben never missed; he always drew blood.

Having completed his devious mission, he would walk off triumphantly, strutting away with the fur standing up along the ridge of his back. You will have spilt your piping hot cup of tea over you and the carpet, leaving you in a distressed condition as you examine the wounds hoping that he hadn't ripped open one of your main arteries. Ben got me quite a few times before I became wise to his charming, conniving, vicious ways. I learned the best way was to ignore him. This turned out to be a good idea. That way, I kept my blood where it belonged.

Another trick of Ben's was to sit halfway up Mother's stairs. This was his watching post. The bad news was the toilet was upstairs, so you had no alternative but to pass by him as he was innocently purring. So, what do you do with a cat that is purring? Well, you do the natural thing. You bend down and stroke the little devil. Who can resist stroking a purring cat?

When you went by him believing you were safe to do so, again he would have led you into a false sense of security. So, what did the little devil do? He would pounce on you and wrap himself around one of your legs, with his back legs kicking and digging in with all his claws out. If you were lucky enough to be wearing jeans, they would help protect you a little bit, but if you had bare legs or wore stockings as most ladies do. Boy, he could inflict some damage and give you some real pain. I think he just about caught everyone out with that little ploy. It was a habit that he never grew out of, and for sure, he had a long list of victims to his name. There was only one way to get up the stairs in one piece, and that was to call my mother to remove him before you set one foot on the stairway. Fortunately, my mother moved to a bungalow, and everyone knows bungalows do not have stairs. So, that was one little trick cuddly Ben was never able to play again.

As Ben grew older, he turned into a real killer. He loved to catch birds and mice, always bringing his trophies back gifted to my mother. Like most cat owners, she loathed him killing the birds in her garden. So, she got him a collar with a bell on it. That initially seemed to do the trick and allowed the bird population to thrive in her garden. But that did not last too long because crafty Ben had an idea.

One afternoon, my mother watched Ben trying to ambush a sparrow, and she could hardly believe her eyes because the crafty little devil was creeping with his chin low, pressing the bell down onto his chest to stop it from ringing. Can you believe that?

Another funny story mother told me about Ben was most certainly what you would call a cat with innovative skills. One morning he came home to present mother with a dead mouse. It was dead all right, but would you believe the mouse came with a mousetrap attached to it? Think about it, why should Ben go to all the effort and trouble chasing a mouse when someone else had done the job for him?

In conclusion, I think you could have stroked Ben for about ten seconds and know you would get away with it. Anytime longer, for sure, you were really pushing your luck. The point that should be coming over from Ben's story is that he had claws, four sets of them as all cats do, and you never knew when he would use them.

Mother loved Ben dearly and fussed over him all the time, but even she wasn't safe from the little horror because occasionally he drew blood from her as well. Even so, she would have nothing said against him. Her excuse was, he had come from a farm and still had the wildness in him.

She was dead right there!

Randy

In my childhood days, we had an enormous cat, and his name was Randy. No, he wasn't named Randy because he was a randy amorous little devil. He was named Randy after a famous boxer Randolph Turpin from my father's day. Randy was a black and brown tabby with a beautiful white blaze running down his face. Because Randy was so overweight when he walked his stomach swayed from side to side, sometimes dragging on the ground. It rubbed away most of his white fur to expose his skin, giving his stomach a pink glow. Can you believe? Randy was twenty-five pounds in weight. No wonder greedy Randy was so big and fat. The crafty devil was being fed elsewhere at three of our next-door neighbour's houses.

Randy often sat sunning himself in his favourite place on the footpath outside our front gate, giving himself a good grooming with his rough pink tongue. One day a black and white mongrel about the size of a Labrador spotted Randy relaxing in the sun. The dog sensing some sport, hurtled toward Randy, expecting him to run, but Randy, unperplexed, just stood his ground to the dog's shock and surprise. He puffed out his fur, and arched his back with his tail high in the air, making him look twice as big. The horrified dog hit the brakes, skidding to a halt with only inches to spare in front of the enormous cat. Suddenly, like greased lightning, Randy swiped his paw just like a left hook from the boxing world, straight across the horrified dog's nose, drawing blood and making him yelp out loud. The cowardly dog rapidly turned and ran whimpering back down the road with its tail between its legs. Randy, totally unconcerned, continued cleaning himself with one of his back legs pointing high in the air just as if nothing had happened.

It didn't take long before the canine race in our neighbourhood learned to respect our giant cat. But I must say, it wasn't just the canine race that respected Randy; it was also the neighbourhood cats. I often noticed both dogs and cats, giving Randy quite a wide berth. And who could blame them?

Jassey

Would a cat take on a large German Shepherd dog? Now that is an excellent question.

I grew up with a German Shepherd dog named Jassey, and she would more than enthusiastically give chase to cats. Jassey was typically marked for the breed and had a black and tan colouring with a beautiful black diamond smack in the middle of her forehead. I suppose she should have been good-looking and handsomely marked because she had a pedigree as long as your arm and had cost my parents a small fortune.

Jassey never bothered Randy, not because he was a great big cat, she just made it obvious that she loved him. They often lay side by side in the sun and in the wintertime by the fire. However, with Jassey, where other cats were concerned, that was most certainly another story.

One sad day, Jassey chased a cat running along the top of the boundary wall in our garden, and as the cat jumped off, she, unfortunately, caught it and killed it within seconds. The unlucky cat belonged to one of our neighbours. That created quite a stir, I can tell you. After that terrible day, we always made sure we kept a close watch on her. Jassey was very obedient, and if we spotted a cat before she did, we made her know in no uncertain terms that the cat was taboo.

Jassey was my constant companion throughout my childhood days. One day when I was walking with her to the local grocery shop, she spotted a cat before I did. Instantly she launched herself like a rocket into the attack. The small cat, which was entirely black, ran like the wind. Not in the opposite direction as I expected, but to my utter amazement, straight at the oncoming giant German Shepherd. It was braver than David taking on Goliath. It certainly looked like the little black cat was going to die in heroic style. And there wasn't a thing I could do about it.

I visualised that small cat disappearing right down Jassey's throat without touching the sides. I also wondered who would be in the most trouble, me or Jassey. The brave hissing, spitting little cat sprang with all four feet in the air like a furry missile with claws extended, straight at the face of Jassey.

I had seen Jassey take on dogs of all shapes and

sizes, and she always won quite easily. She had also killed hundreds of rats, almost the same size as the little black cat. Even Jassey was no match for the flying little black bundle of spitting fury accompanied by teeth and hooked claws. To my disbelief, the giant German Shepherd turned tail and fled for her life.

I just stood rooted to the spot as I watched in awe as the brave little cat gave chase with her hackles up and tail in the air. The little cat chased Jassey at least fifty yards as she ran yelping with her tail between her legs. I started laughing until I could hardly stand up. It was just like watching a Tom and Jerry cartoon. I could not believe that the little black cat had been so brave. And it wasn't long before I found out why?

When I eventually walked into the grocer's shop, I told the proprietor, Mr Johnson, what had happened and how I could not believe what I had witnessed. He informed me that the little black cat belonged to him and had given birth to six kittens two weeks before. Is that what you call a protective mother, or what? Maternal instincts were undoubtedly running high that day. That's for sure.

Over the years, cats have drawn blood from me on quite a few occasions and thankfully, it was with their claws and not their teeth! Dogs have never been much of a problem, even though some of them could have been twenty times bigger than my little friend Mr Tiddles.

If you take a Jack Russell and a similar-sized cat, which one would you fancy your chances against if it came at you in full attack mode? Also, if cats were the same size as Rottweilers, they would compare to leopards.

Need I say more? My case rests there!

CHAPTER 11

Tiger On The Loose

Another interesting cat story and why my lovely enclosed shrubbery in the cattery building had to go.

One morning, I was called down to the cattery because the girls could not find a so-called 'dangerous' cat named Tiger. Apparently, he had sneaked out when they were cleaning his run. They thought he had hidden in the enclosed shrubbery that was surrounded by a cream-tiled path. And just to make things worse he was a well-camouflaged tabby cat. Also, clipped on the outside of Tiger's galvanised steel mesh gate was a label in large writing, in the usual blood-red:

STRIKES OUT WITHOUT ANY WARNING

During his stay, Tiger had ruined many a pair of rubber gloves as the cattery girls cautiously worked around him. It was fortunate that they were wearing gloves for cleaning, or it would have been their hands that took the hit. But I must say, a rubber glove does not give much protection from a cat's razor-sharp claws.

The girls had been looking for Tiger for over thirty minutes. Amy was the girl taking care of

Tiger, and she was very concerned.

I asked,

“Amy, are you sure he hasn’t escaped through the main gate?”

She replied,

“No. Other than coming for you, none of us have been out of the cattery. We are sure he is hiding in the shrubbery.”

I absorbed her information, but I did not let on how worried I was.

'Please let him be in the shrubbery and not outside. Please, please, don’t do this to me.’

If I walked and crawled up and down that shrubbery once, I did it a hundred times. I was certain Tiger was not in the shrubbery.

‘Oh no! He's gone!'

I had been searching for Tiger for more than half an hour. Considering the shrubbery was only forty feet long and eight feet wide, there was no way he could still be hiding in it. By then, I knew every leaf on every shrub in that bit of enclosed garden.

'This shrubbery is going as soon as I get around to it. I am not putting up with this stressful time-wasting anymore.'

I searched and searched, but still no Tiger.

'What on earth am I going to do? How do I break the news to his owners?'

I decided to check out his run.

'Maybe, just maybe, he has wandered back in.'

I could only hope for a miracle.

There were fifteen runs on each side of the shrubbery. The gate in question was number seven, which just happens to be my lucky number. I walked along the cream-tiled path down the side of the shrubbery and reached Tiger's run. The mesh gate was slightly ajar. In hope, I crossed my fingers and looked in but there was no sign of him. I went in carefully, closing the gate behind me just in case he was hiding inside his enclosed litter tray. I peered inside.

'Arghh! No Tiger!'

I gently lifted the lid of his cream-plastic sleeping box. And yes, yes, yes, to my relief, there he was curled up fast asleep on his owner's pink jumper. I looked at him, contently sleeping and noticed that his four feet were twitching. I thought he was probably dreaming about playing hide and seek with my girls in the shrubbery. Or more than likely, me!

I just could not believe my eyes. I could have kissed the little devil even if he could have swiped out at me. My thoughts of Tiger being a dangerous cat had gone clean out of my head, and so had the time I had wasted. Thank you very much, my lucky number seven.

So, this is what I believe happened. When the girls were away from the cattery giving me the bad news, Tiger had slipped out of the shrubbery back into his bed. Why on earth didn't I look in the obvious place in the first instance? So, this episode was the last straw. That is why the shrubbery had to go.

Who would think tranquil things like shrubs could give you so much stress?

The Shrubbery

The shrubbery ran down the middle of the cattery and caused many problems over the first two years, even though it looked very nice. It made the cattery look quite tranquil. This was an excellent selling point, especially when prospective customers came down to inspect where their loved ones might eventually stay.

Cattery and kennel buildings are a bit like prisons. I am afraid that is the way they must be. It is not a good idea to have any chance of an escape route that the ambitious escapee might find. My idea of the shrubbery was to soften the steel and mesh making the cattery look less stark. After a couple of years the shrubs had thrived and grown far more than I had anticipated. I purchased them from a local garden centre, supposedly as dwarf shrubs. No way were they dwarf shrubs.

The so-called dwarf shrubs had grown into what I could only describe as a mini-jungle. They had spread over the cream-coloured Cotswold gravel that I had painstakingly spread between the shrubs and then overflowed onto the cream-tiled walkway. Also, cat hair lodged between the gravel, making it very difficult to pick up. Our unwanted jungle's worst problem was with the cats that had dodged around staff members when they were cleaning them out. It wasn't any cause for major concern because there was no escape route because of the mesh roof above and the extra security door on the outside of the building.

As with Tiger, the most challenging task we had was locating any mischievous cats hidden in the jungle, sorry, I mean shrubbery. Locating a white cat was no problem, but trying to find a well-camouflaged tabby was an absolute nightmare. When we eventually found a missing cat, we had to catch it without getting scratched and bitten and return it to the correct run. No easy task in some cases. Maybe the staff did not have fun playing hide and seek, but I am sure many of the escapees did. Sometimes it was as time-consuming as trying to find a 'needle in a haystack'. I didn't need to be a rocket scientist to realise that it wasted time and time was costing us money.

I have never been one to hang about once I have made a decision. The shrubs had been growing for over two years and had done exceptionally well. That made the job of digging them up even harder. They were in beautiful condition and I did not want to throw them away. My idea was to replant the shrubs in the large lawn area between the cattery building and the kennel block and office. The work was tough going, but I managed to dig all the shrubs up and replant them. I must say, when my hard work was completed, they did look rather lovely, dotted about on the mowed lawn between the two buildings.

Once the shrubs were re-planted, I used to have fun whipping around them on my red Wheelhorse tractor mower, almost as if they were slalom gates on a ski run. Before I re-planted the shrubs, I used to contentedly ride the mower in the hot sunshine. Occasionally, I would momentarily dose off resulting in a kink interrupting my near-perfect straight lines. Therefore, the benefit of the slalom action kept me wide awake getting rid of those sleepy tell-tale kinks.

Removing the shrubs left a large unsightly space with numerous holes in the middle of the cattery. I most certainly did not want customers to see that, so I quickly levelled it and filled it with ready-mix concrete. More cream tiles needed laying, so out came my knee pads. After a bout of sore knees, my alterations turned out to be a great success, and it certainly made the cattery look a lot larger, cleaner, and tidier. Also, it made a lot more space for the girls to work.

To soften the blow of any starkness, I hung colourful baskets of busy lizzies and petunias from the mesh roof, adding to the ones already hanging there. Kathy's talented mother, Isabelle, made all the hanging baskets each year and they always looked beautiful. The cattery girls even wore carpet slippers to keep the tiles spotlessly clean.

Once I had re-straightened my back after laying the cream tiles, I decided to build an enclosed area outside the entrance of the cattery. I designed a 12 x 12-foot steel mesh cage that I bolted to the outside of the building. This added extra security to the entrance and incorporated an attractive two-tone green fibreglass shed that stored cat food, cleaning equipment and a workplace for the staff to prepare cat food.

This resulted in triple security. No cat could slip out of my cattery now.

Would those be my famous last words? Mind you, with the previous double security we had never lost a cat.

My motto was, 'Never be over cautious'.

You never know what is around the corner, especially when dealing with other people's pets.

Unfortunately, around the corner happened.

But that is a future story.

CHAPTER 12

Percy's Amazing Trick

A practical joker and his dog.

Percy was a West Highland Terrier, we called them Westies for short. And boy, he was a little chap I will most certainly never forget. His owner was a humorous character and just happened to be in the British police force. The first time I met Percy's 'dad,' Mr Hughes, he turned up in a police patrol car, coloured white with a red stripe along its side. In those days, some people referred to them as 'Jam Butty cars'. Maybe they still do.

I was sitting comfortably in my plush green leather captain's chair (a birthday present from Kathy) sorting out paperwork on the desk in the study. Kathy was dusting and polishing upstairs on the landing.

She looked out of the window and shouted,

"HEY, GEOFF! There's a police car on the car park. I think it might be a good idea to go and see what he wants."

I looked out the study window, thinking Kathy was joking, but sure enough, on the car park was a police patrol car, and walking towards the kennel office was a rather large rotund uniformed policeman.

'Oh no! I've been recorded for speeding. He's come to deliver the fine.'

It would not have been a surprise because I was always rushing about in some sort of emergency. It could have been a journey to the vets or getting some supplies for the business. It would have been my first speeding offence, so I supposed I had done pretty well to get away with it for so long. Surely the speeding offence wouldn't be for Miss, 'Goody Two Shoes' (Kathy). Mind you, she had been caught once already, and I just cannot resist deviating for a few minutes to tell this short story.

A few days before a Christmas break, Kathy was driving along in her posh new white Toyota Celica with Margaret, a friend from work. They had been collecting the Christmas raffle prizes for their work draw at Barclays. Margaret had been informing Kathy all about the latest office gossip. Kathy was oblivious to the fact that a police patrol car had been following her for well over a mile in a built-up area virtually on her back bumper. She had been speeding at fifteen miles per hour over the speed limit. As pretty as she was and still is (I have to put that in, don't I?), she couldn't persuade the police officer to wavier the booking.

This is the bit I find amusing...

She arrived home quite disgruntled and said,

"He even had the gall to wish me a Happy Christmas!"

I joked,

"Hey Kathy, it might be an idea to check the rear-view mirror now and again."

By the stone-cold look she gave me, I don't think she appreciated that comment one little bit.

Well, back to the plot and maybe my speeding problem. I wasn't as good-looking as Kathy, so I stood very little chance of getting away with a booking fine. So, I decided it would be better to go and face the music and get it over and done with.

As I approached the kennel block, I could hear laughter coming from the office. The policeman was talking to Pat, and I thought it couldn't be anything too serious, especially if there was humour in the air.

And what a pleasant surprise I had.

The rotund uniformed policeman had a ruddy face sporting gold wire-rim spectacles. He was very cheerful and said he had been recommended to us. He just happened to be passing by the entrance to our drive, so he thought it would be a good idea to pop in and inspect the kennels for his dog Percy. He was very impressed and said that he would let us know when he knew the dates. Little did I know that Percy would become one of our most memorable and regular guests.

One sunny morning, Percy's 'dad' surprised us yet again when he turned up riding a powerful police patrol motorbike. He had his dates and booked Percy's first stay with us.

As he was leaving, he laughed and said,

"I suppose I will have to go out and see if I can make someone's day."

Meaning book someone for speeding or other

driving offence!

Does that statement remind you of the famous Dirty Harry movie starring Clint Eastwood?

After those famous Clint words, Mr Hughes roared off on his patrol bike. He had laughter all over his round pink humorous face. I often wondered what would have happened if the laughing policeman had caught me speeding, especially after I had become such a good friend of Percy's. Would he have let me go with a friendly caution?

When the laughing policeman eventually delivered Percy, he drove a regular run-of-the-mill car, for all I knew, maybe an unmarked police car. Percy loved coming to us, and we loved having him. He never looked back to his cheerful owner as he stood watching with hands on hips. All Percy was interested in was getting into the wood as soon as possible, where all those delightful smells were waiting to titillate his little shiny black nose. But for anybody new walking him, he had a little surprise waiting for them, hiding up his sleeve, you might say.

Yes, Percy could most certainly make your day. It would be a day to remember alright because he had a very unusual habit. In fact, we never saw another dog in all the years of running our boarding establishment come close to the fantastic trick of Percy's. I don't know if I was fortunate or unfortunate to be the first one to find out about it. I just happened to be the first person to walk him on his first day. I thought walking Percy would impress his dad, the big laughing policeman, especially if Geoff, the boss of the best pet hotel in Great Britain, walked the dogs as well. I also thought he might recommend his police pals to use our facilities, and sure enough, that is what he did.

As I set off around the wood with Percy safely attached to his lead, I noticed he was thoroughly enjoying himself, strutting away, looking quite important. Maybe he thought he was a police dog? I was totally engrossed in watching Percy. Suddenly, with no warning whatsoever, Percy did a handstand. I thought that was a good trick for a circus dog, but his trick got even better. As his two back legs were waving up at the sky and the other more handsome end, meaning his face was contemplating the other side of the world, maybe Australia. A powerful jet of dog pee shot straight out like a bullet from the secret pistol that lived between Percy's legs.

ARRRRRGH!

Not in any way expecting this unlikely stunt on that cold day, a jet of soothingly warm dog pee hit me full blast in my left ear. To say I was shocked was a gross understatement. I was dumbfounded and was not too amused either. The last thing I needed was to have my left ear syringed by dog pee. What is more, I had only had my ears syringed by my doctor the week before. I looked down at Percy in amazement as I groped in my pocket for a handkerchief. Thank goodness I had one with me.

Percy looked up at me as he wagged his little docked tail (and I don't mean the one that had just squirted me in my ear) as if to say,

"Come on Geoff. Stop dawdling. Let's get on with my walk."

Percy wasn't malicious in any way, and I am sure he had no idea what he had done.

'I bet that laughing policeman knows all about Percy's little trick. And he is laughing all the way down our drive.'

As far as I knew, the laughing policeman had not told anyone else (my staff) about Percy's little trick. So why should I? What a naughty devious thought. The last thing I wanted was my staff taking the Mickey out of me because Percy had peed in my ear. To say they would take the pee would have been an understatement. No, I decided not to tell a soul, especially my manager Pat.

Then I had a naughty thought,

'Let nature take its natural course.'

Or should I,

'Let Percy take aim.'

It was mid-morning when I had taken Percy on that more than memorable first walk, so when he was due to be taken out for the late afternoon walk, I would wangle that it would be Pat who would walk him. Pat had played a few practical jokes on me in the past, and this was going to be payback.

Big time!

After trying my best to clean and dry out my smelly cooling ear, I completed Percy's more than memorable first walk and led him to his allocated kennel.

I stroked his head and whispered,

"May your aim be true this afternoon little chap?"

I went into the office to see Pat and smiled not too mischievously as I said,

"Make sure you walk Percy this afternoon and give him your very best attention, especially with his owner being a policeman. Anyway, it is the perk of the job being able to walk a nice little dog like that. Why be dragged around the wood with the usual lunatics that pull your arms out of their sockets?"

She smiled at me, and I knew I had sold her the job of walking Percy. In the latter years, as the business thrived, I didn't always help with dog walking, especially in the afternoons. But I most certainly put myself in a position to make sure I was available to help on that afternoon.

Dog walking began at the usual time of 4 pm, and my fair lady friend Pat put Percy on his lead. I took the dog from the next run to Percy's to enable me to follow, or should I say 'tail' Pat and watch the little chap in action.

Pat said,

"How come we have your rare presence for this afternoon's dog walking?"

Deviously, I replied,

"Oh, I finished doing that bit of painting at the back of the cattery quicker than I expected and fancied giving you a hand and get some exercise."

Hearing my reply, she just gave me a puzzled look, so in great anticipation, I followed her with a Golden Retriever that was almost yanking me off my feet. I was about fifteen yards behind, waiting for the action. But to my immense disappointment, Percy stopped and cocked his back leg just like any other dog and had a little pee. There was no handstand to be seen anywhere.

'What is going on? What's gone wrong? Is Percy taking the pee or what? Have I imagined it? No, I don't think so. I would remember his warm dog pee penetrating my inner ear for the rest of my life.'

Ignoring my disappointment, I carried on following the pair from a discreet distance, and suddenly with no warning for my intended victim, Percy went up onto his front legs into a perfect handstand that an Olympic gymnast would have been proud of.

'Here goes. Good old Percy.'

A jet of yellow pee shot out from Percy's secret pistol and hit his unsuspecting victim splattering the side of her neck.

'Not bad Percy. But it would have been better in her ear.'

I suppose beggars can't be choosers. I nearly keeled over with laughter. On hearing me, Pat turned around and gave me the filthiest look possible; obviously, she had not seen the funny side of Percy's stunt.

She shouted,

"GEOFF, YOU SWINE! I thought it was unusual that you were helping with the dog walking. You knew he was going to do that. Didn't you?"

'Not the way to talk to your boss. But maybe I deserved it.'

I tried to keep a straight face as I said,

"Who? Me? Now, what makes you think I would do a thing like that?"

I could see my little prank did not amuse Pat one little bit as she tried to wipe Percy's cooling pee from her neck with the sleeve of her blue pullover.

I could not prevent a smirk from forming on my face as I said,

"Hey Pat, do you want to borrow my handkerchief?"

I was sure I could see the hint of a wry smile on her face.

She said,

"Don't you worry Geoff? You won't get away with this. I will never forget how you tricked me into taking Percy for a walk. I'll get you back one of these days. You just wait and see."

I retaliated with a little white lie and said,

"I didn't know Percy was going to get you like that. Anyway, are you forgetting the Benny boy episode? As they say in the bible, 'An eye for an eye'."

Pat remained silent and just answered with a chilling glare.

'Oh no! What's she going to come up with next?'

Anyway, that's enough of my amusing war with Pat, let's get back to Percy the star of this story.

Percy's fame spread far and wide, or should I say rapidly amongst the staff. They made sure that when they walked him, they were very vigilant and not in the firing line when he did his numerous handstands and shot his little pistol. I deviously told the staff a little white lie. I said that Percy had just missed me when I first walked him. I kept mine and Percy's dark secret for a long time.

After all, it could have been much more than my life was worth if Pat had learned the truth.

Percy always came to us spotlessly white, which never lasted too long. After he had been around the wood a few times, his white stomach turned yellow because his frequent handstands made his pee trickle down his upturned tummy. The pee made Percy's undercarriage damp, and when his paws flicked up the dry, dusty brown peaty woodland soil, it stuck to his hair. Each day Percy lost some of his whiteness and turned more and more yellowy-brown. So, on the day he was collected, the girls always bathed him, and he was once again transformed into a bright fluffy little white Westie, ready for the laughing policeman to pick him up.

I often wondered if the laughing policeman, 'made someone's day' when he was on holiday.

CHAPTER 13

The Disgusting Problem Of Stinking Dogs

Did you notice the tiny mouse showering under the chair?

This is a story about our kennel maids in their element.

It did not take us long to realise that when dogs stayed with us, there was a good chance they could smell when they were being collected. Smell is not even the operative word here because they could absolutely stink, or even honk would be a more appropriate description. The smell some dogs acquired was no fault of yours truly or our conscientious staff because we kept the kennels spotlessly clean. But we could not keep them clean twenty-four hours a day. That would have been impossible.

So, why did some dogs stink or honk if our kennels were so clean? Well, the reason they smelt so bad was they were peeing and crapping throughout the night and sitting in it before we were able to clean the mess up the following morning. Most dogs didn't sit in their crap too much, but they sat in their pee, and I mean big time. They used to pee in their runs, sit in it, lie in it, or even roll in it! The dogs were usually of the male variety, bitches were generally much cleaner and would patiently wait for their walks in the morning.

Each run's concrete floor had a slight fall sloping down from the sleeping quarters to a mesh gate. My idea was to allow any smelly dog pee to trickle down the concrete to an open gulley on the other side of the slightly raised galvanised steel mesh framework and gate. Unfortunately, up against the mesh and gate is precisely where most dogs preferred lying. With this in mind, I designed unique steel-framed carbon fibre benches to fit right up against the mesh gates to combat this major problem. My idea was to raise the resting dogs off the floor, making them more comfortable. But more importantly, pee from higher up the run could flow or seep underneath the benches into the gully on the other side of the gate. Therefore, the dog's coats would not get soiled. But did they use them? Did they heck!

Many dogs just ignored my benches and lay in their pee higher up the run. And boy, oh boy, they didn't half-whiff after they had been with us for a few days. Nobody in their right mind would have wanted to cuddle those smelly creatures, especially when they had been staying with us for a couple of weeks or more, that's for sure.

Can you imagine what those canines would smell like in a confined space, such as a car on their way home? Not only would you smell the stench, but you would probably be able to see it in the air as well! I would hate to think what it would be like riding along with the obnoxious smell getting worse and worse by the second. I can assure you it would become disgustingly unbearable.

The owners would most certainly have blamed us for the state of their best friend's obnoxious aroma, which was wafting from its coat—no doubt about it. We had to sort out the immense smelly problem once and for all because I knew we would get a very bad or even smelly name for our thriving business.

So how do we solve this massive problem? Yes, bathe the dogs. That is the answer. And that is just what we did. Even a clean dog that had been with us for more than two days was automatically bathed because it could have developed a natural doggy odour, which all dogs eventually do. Dogs sweat just like humans and like humans; unfortunately, some smell much more potent than others.

I mentioned automatically bathed, but we didn't have a machine like a dishwasher, called a dog washer. Perhaps I should have invented one. No, the girls did the bathing, and they thoroughly enjoyed it too. That is the girls, not the dogs! But most of the dogs did enjoy it. There was only a minority that was not too keen. And guess what? They were usually the ones that needed bathing the most.

Some of our regular guests enjoyed being bathed so much I am sure they got dirty on purpose just to get another bath before they went home. Occasionally, some dogs within minutes of their nice warm bath would roll in the mud when we walked them; we just couldn't seem to stop them. Hey ho, more work for the girls. So, they bathed the little blighters again.

Once this had happened a few times, we got wise to them and in wet weather we stopped walking those clean hounds in the wood and took them down our tarmac drive instead. So that was yet another major problem solved. I am sure some of the dogs left our premises cleaner than when they came in.

Tiny

An English Mastiff boarded with us called TINY. Now that is an excellent humorous name because the English Mastiff is a gigantic breed.

Dog fact time again folks!

The skinny Irish wolfhound is classed as the tallest globally, but the largest, bulkiest, and heaviest award goes to the English Mastiff.

The English Mastiff is the largest dog breed globally by considering the mass. This breed has an average weight of 150-240 pounds and a shoulder height of 27-3 inches. On 26th September 1981, the Guinness Book of world records recognised an old English Mastiff named Zorba as the world's heaviest and longest dog.

At fifteen months old, TINY was almost full-grown but already he was a giant of a dog. He was quite easily the biggest dog I had ever seen. You could compare him to a donkey or even a young giraffe with a short neck. And it took three girls to bathe him.

TINY was so big he couldn't even fit in the kennel bath in our grooming parlour, which was the standard design and size for human usage, so perhaps that puts his size into perspective. The only way the girls could shampoo him was outside on the grass. The three girls, Hannah, Tracey, Haley, and the enormous TINY, made a lovely picture on a warm summer's day.

One girl stood on a chair showering him with a hosepipe, as the second girl tended to his every need and the third girl held on to his lead. He just stood there with a daft expression on his face, and I must say he did appear to enjoy himself. One amused customer who was here collecting her dog took photographs of the memorable event.

Sam

One of our customers had a white Samoyed, and I am sure you would never have guessed what his name was. Yes, yet another Sam. How about that for originality? The first time Sam's owners collected him, they thought we had brought out the wrong dog because he was so white and fluffy. Not only had the girls bathed him, but they had groomed him as well.

When we bathed the dogs (or should I say the girls did), they used shampoo meant for humans; what a rip-off dog shampoo was. It was an exorbitant price for only a small container. I soon came up with a much cheaper idea...

Human Shampoo!

I travelled twenty-five miles to a wholesaler in Stoke-on-Trent, who provided a service for the hairdressing shops in the area. I used to go into the large warehouse and purchase twenty-five, or maybe thirty, one gallon (5 litres) containers of shampoo and as a bonus, it came in all sorts of exotic perfumes too. It was never possible to get all the shampoo in the same fragrance because we always needed so much. I would telephone first to make sure they had enough stock. The lemon scent was my personal favourite, but it also came in almond, apple, orange, passion fruit, peach, pear, and strawberry, to name a few. And even bubble gum, can you believe?

Bubble gum! Bubble gum! Who the heck in their right mind would want the scent of bubble gum in their hair?

Initially, the warehouse owner thought I had a chain of hairdressing shops because I was there so often; it was a big surprise when I informed him the shampoo was for dogs. He looked at me in disbelief and eventually realised I wasn't taking the 'Mickey'. He found it quite amusing I was using human shampoo on dogs. I should imagine TINY'S fur coat would have added up to the equivalent of at least thirty heads of human hair. We used at least half a pint of shampoo on his coat, and that was no exaggeration when a tablespoon would have been more than enough for us humans.

Occasionally, when the girls were short of work, I asked them to wash my Toyota Land Cruiser. I could never understand why they always moaned at me because they needed a chair to stand on. They never moaned when they stood on a chair and bathed TINY, which used to take them at least three times longer. And in the process, especially with TINY, they got themselves extremely wet. At least the Land Cruiser didn't shake its coat all over them like TINY did, soaking them even more and creating sounds of girlie squeals and laughter. Well, I suppose the answer was bathing an English Mastiff was much more fun than the boss's boring Land Cruiser.

When the girls had finished a good bathing session, I sometimes wondered if the dogs had bathed the girls who appeared to be far wetter.

After the customers had happily collected their recently shampooed sweet-smelling perfumed pooches, they often rang up and congratulated us on how beautiful their dog looked and smelt.

As far as I was concerned, SMELT was the keyword!

Numerous customers came up with the same sentence,

“Is that lovely smell from the disinfectant you use?”

“No, we have shampooed your dog.”

“Really, that’s incredible. He never lets us shampoo him.”

Say no more!

The free shampooing service we provided increased our trade, and we never informed the owners that we had bathed their dogs because sometimes they might have wanted to know the reason why.

They might have said,

“But why did you bathe him?”

My reply could have been,

"Oh, because he likes lying in his crap and pee."

I am sure they would have loved to learn about that kennel secret! Am I kidding, or what?

Anyway, how the heck could I tell the owners that their sweet *'Rover'* was the filthiest dog in the kennels?

Some dogs got bathed because they had a slobber problem. What I mean is, they would have saliva drooling, or even worse, at times, it would be wrapped around their jaws like slimy cling film. YUK!!!

Those breeds were usually dogs with big jowls like Bulldogs, Great Danes, Rottweilers and especially Boxers. We always had to keep our eye on dogs like that, not because they were dangerous, but if they shook their heads, the slobber hanging six inches from their jowls could quickly fly and hit you on the side of your face, attaching itself in a cold, wet, horrible slimy string, or if you were unlucky...

On, or in your mouth!

Now that was one good reason to keep your mouth well and truly closed. Not a very pleasant prospect, believe me. So those slobbery, slimy characters needed a good clean-up as well. Good luck, girls, rather you than me!

The afternoon before a busy collection day, the girls bathed as many as forty dogs. It was just like a conveyer belt of dogs passing the office on their way to the grooming parlour and clipping room. Yes, we did clipping as well! A dirty dog bouncing all over the place would go past the office door, not knowing what was in store for him. He probably thought he was going out for another walk in the wood, albeit in a different direction. But straight into the grooming parlour, he went.

Most dogs enjoyed the rough and tumble with the girls. Only a few found having a bath was not quite to their liking. The staff members would decide on the day whether they were in the bathing team or the drying team.

After the bathing team had bathed each dog, they gave the wet, bedraggled dog to the drying team. The drying team waited in anticipation to find how boisterous the next dog would be —depending on the dog's coat, dried with hair-driers or on the lawn with towels.

Fortunately, it was usually the summer when the hectic bathing days took place. So, with lots of rubs from the towel and many violent shakes from the dog, they would soon be dry. It was no wonder the girls got soaked because when a dog shakes the water from its coat it goes everywhere. Watched in slow motion, it resembles a revolving spin dryer. We always prayed the sun would be shining on the mega-busy days.

It wasn't long before the dogs looked like they were about to be shown at Crufts. The dogs would be clean, fluffy and, more importantly, smelling sweetly from the perfumed shampoo, whichever the girls had fancied using on the day. Maybe it was bubble gum!

Were those lucky dogs pampered or what?

I often watched all this action with a big grin on my face. The girls were happy; the dogs were happy; the owners were happy.

And, of course, Geoff's big nose and his keen sense of smell was more than happy.

CHAPTER 14

The Incredible Adventures Of Mother

These hilarious stories feature my mum. So, why not save the best till last? Especially the final story about a Bulldog named Fred.

It is an absolute classic!

My Mum's name is Irene. In this chapter, I have referred to her as Mother, with a capital M!

I have to say that Mick's caricature of Mother is not a bad likeness.

When writing this book, Mother had two cats, Ben and Jimmy. She also had a dog, a small Border Collie cross named Zoe. My sister Gail also had many animals ranging from cats, dogs, horses, goats and even a large snail in a jar, let alone other small animals that she collected over the years. At times, it appeared that Gail was well on the way to having a small zoo. So, do you get the idea that my family love animals?

In the initial years, Mother and Gail helped at the pet hotel, but this story is all about the incredible adventures of Mother.

Mother had always loved animals, so she couldn't wait to help us when we opened the pet hotel. To coin a phrase, 'she was chomping at the bit'. Mother was in her early sixties, well sixty-two but she certainly didn't look it. And her energy levels were like someone twenty years younger. All her family were long-lived; her mother was still alive at that time, my grandmother being twenty-three years Mother's senior. I will let you do the calculation on that one.

Mother wore glasses and was only five feet tall, making people think she looked a lot younger. She was very fit for her age and keen to help us in any way possible. Not only did she love being with the animals, but as a bonus it would keep her fitter and younger.

Mother loved to help us with the dog walking and went onto the payroll, just like any other staff member. And for sure, you can't get anyone more reliable than your mum. Well, Mother certainly was very reliable in turning up for the dog walking, and she was always smack on time and raring to go.

But how reliable was she at walking dogs?

Mother certainly turned out to be very reliable indeed, especially at making us laugh with her many adventures whilst dog walking. We used to give her the dogs that were easiest to walk and unlikely to pull her over. Could you imagine giving my five feet nothing Mother, two German Shepherds to walk? It doesn't bear thinking about!

I emphasised, or should I say, I virtually brainwashed her, stating on numerous occasions,

"Whatever happens, Mum. You must never, ever let go of the lead!"

I knew if we had given Mother two German Shepherds to walk, she would have ended up face down on her stomach hanging onto their leads at ten miles per hour. Mother would certainly have been around that woodland walk in record time. So no, we just gave her little dogs which she could manage, such as Yorkshire Terriers, Jack Russells, and West Highland Terriers.

So, here comes Mother's first adventure.

Jess And Emma

But, after a few weeks of being a very successful dog walker, Mother had ambitions.

BIG AMBITIONS!

Ambitions in the form of two placid yellow Labrador bitches called Jess and Emma. Probably because she had always wanted a Labrador of her own. And at that time, it looked like she was hoping for a chance of two. The largest dogs Mother had walked together were two Westies. I don't know how, but she managed to persuade me to let her walk the two yellow Labs. Sales talk obviously runs in the family. At least I knew they did not pull on their leads.

So, off my lovely bright-eyed bushy-tailed Mother proudly strutted, full of her new self-importance along with Jess and Emma. As she left the kennels, I hoped the stern warning I had brainwashed her with was still ringing in her ears.

"Whatever happens, Mum. You must never, ever let go of the lead!"

I asked the other staff who were walking guests at the same time to keep a watchful eye on her. Anyway, Jess and Emma were well-trained gundogs, and I knew they were very obedient. So, there shouldn't be any problems at all.

Or so I thought!

The first time Mother walked the Labs, there was nothing for me to worry about because she came back with a big grin on her face after completing the circuit in the wood. With that successful jaunt under her belt Mother was eager to take out two more large dogs for walks. But I decided not to push our luck, or should I say Mother's luck too far. With great disappointment, she shrugged and went back to walking smaller dogs.

The dog walking was certainly keeping Mother very fit, and she had no problem doing the circuit at least ten times twice a day. Every day she enjoyed herself so much with Jess and Emma that she insisted on being the person to take them out. And why not? It was inevitable that everyone had their favourites, including me, so that was okay with the rest of the staff because they could also choose. And sure enough, they did.

But inevitably, one afternoon, disaster struck.

To my astonishment, Jess and Emma ran back into the kennels dragging their leads behind them.

Surprise, surprise!

No Mother attached to the other end.

Jess and Emma were okay. But, more importantly, where the heck was Mother?

With that, I ran into the wood, trying hard not to imagine what catastrophe might have befallen her. I had only gone about twenty yards along the woodland path when something I can only describe as a black apparition appeared before me. The only way the thing standing before me resembled Mother was its height. Other than that, it looked like a frightening apparition from the bog. But, sure enough, it was Mother. She looked like some sort of mud monster. Only this monster wasn't very frightening at all because it was sadly sobbing.

I rushed up to her and said,

"Are you ok, Mum?"

Through her intermittent sobs, she said,

"Yes, but Geoffrey, I let go of their leads."

'Mum always uses my full name when the issue is serious.'

"Hey Mum, don't worry, Jess and Emma are ok. They're back in the kennels."

I could see Mother's face brighten up with the good news.

Mother looked a rare old sight. One lens of her glasses was blocked with mud, and her fine white hair had turned almost black with copious amounts of mud clinging to it. I could tell Mother had been dragged a fair distance because her clothes were also covered in peaty woodland mud, and one of her green wellington boots was missing. Thankfully, she wasn't hurt but just a little shaken and I won't talk about her pride.

I am sorry, but I couldn't help myself. I started

laughing,

“Ha! Ha! Ha! Ha! Ha!”

And it wasn’t long before she started to laugh with me.

We laughed until we nearly cried. Thank goodness mother could see the funny side of her misadventure. I wiped the tears of mirth from my eyes with my big white handkerchief.

I said,

“I’ve just got to take a photograph of you.”

And we both laughed even more.

It turned out that a cock pheasant had run out in front of the two Labradors, and of course, being gundogs, they couldn’t resist their instinct. Ignoring their master’s strict training, not to chase after game unless instructed, Jess and Emma bolted simultaneously after the speeding pheasant, yanking poor old Mother clean off her feet. She had hung on desperately, leaving one wellie (wellington boot) behind in the sticky mud. But true to her promise, Mother had gamely hung on to the two leads for as long as possible. She had remembered what my strict explicit instructions were and had been very brave hanging on for at least ten yards. I could see her skid marks in the mud to prove it. Ten yards is an awful long way to be dragged by two Labradors in their prime whilst lying face down in the mud.

To this day, Mother still holds that ten-yard record for a different form of drag racing. A record that I am sure will never get broken.

Interesting Fact:

The Wellington boot is named after Arthur Wellesley, 1st Duke of Wellington who wore and popularised this boot style. Originally, it was a type of hessian military riding boot, later made from leather. The Wellington boot became the staple practical footwear for the British aristocracy during their country pursuits. Subsequently, the name was given to waterproof boots made from rubber.

Geoff Fact:

When we were kids, using Shropshire slang, we called them wellies!

Bill

Another dog that Mother walked many times became one of her firm favourites. It was an adorable little black mongrel called Bill.

One morning walk, Mother came wandering back to the kennels with Bill's lead and collar trailing behind her...

But no Bill!

Either Bill had turned invisible, or he had disappeared over the horizon. I rapidly assessed it had to be the latter, but at least she had hung onto his lead as instructed. But where the heck was Bill? To this day, I don't think she even knew Bill wasn't behind her at the end of his collar and lead. Mother had proudly walked into the kennels—Bill less!

I looked at Mother in unbelieving wonder and said,

"Where is Bill?"

She looked back at me in amazement and then turned round to where little Bill should have been. I didn't have time to wait for her answer. Instead, I just dashed straight past her to make my frequent sprint to the boundary five-bar gate to try and seal Bill's escape route.

'Here, we go again!'

Before I got back from my fruitless sprint, good old prodigal Bill had returned under his own steam, none the worse for wear. He didn't need Mother, or anyone else for that matter, to show him the way back to his temporary home.

Many of our friends enjoying a drink or dinner with us, have had many a laugh over Mother walking an empty collar and lead.

Beauty

Another little story about a dog Mother used to walk, which she became very fond of. This dog was an old black Labrador called Beauty, owned by a couple of friends. Beauty was lovely-natured and would not hurt a fly, she fell totally in love with Mother and vice versa. Unfortunately, Beauty was way, way overweight, which is a notable factor in this story. Being overweight is quite common for old Labradors. I am afraid their owners always spoil them by giving them extra food and treats, which they could well have done without. Most Labradors eat very quickly, almost turning themselves into canine vacuum cleaners, sucking up their food as quickly as possible.

And Beauty was a prime example!

Beauty was an ideal walk for Mother because she was very slow, being old and fat! (I mean Beauty, not my Mother!) So, Mother walked her every time, and they became good friends. Beauty took to Mother like a duck to water, just as if she was her new owner. As they walked around the wood, Beauty would non-stop nuzzle Mother's legs and hands making walking awkward.

One morning, at least twenty minutes must have gone by before the staff realised that there was no Mother, and even worse…

No Beauty!

Having experienced more than a few stressful moments with Mother, my manager thought it should be up to me to search for her. After all, she was my Mother. So off I went to look for the dynamic pair.

'Heck, this brings back memories. What will I find this time?'

Anyway, it wasn't long before I located both of them, and I will never forget the sight that beheld me. Mother was lying flat on her back. But she wasn't alone because big, fat Beauty was sitting proudly on Mother's chest.

I just couldn't believe what I was seeing. Mother was laughing, and I could see Beauty thought it was some sort of game. Her tail was wagging furiously, and she was trying to lick Mother's face. With the weight of Beauty on her chest, Mother couldn't even move, let alone get up.

Then Mother spotted me laughing.

She half screamed and laughed at the same time,

"GEOFFREY."

"Get this dog off me now. She's crushing me to death!"

'Here we go again, using my full name!'

I couldn't resist saying,

"You'll have to wait. I'm going to get my camera."

I certainly wished I had a camera with me at that moment in time to record the extraordinary event.

Mother yelled back, half-laughing,

"You dare, just you dare. GEOFFREY! GEOFFREY! You come back here right now and get this blasted dog off me!"

Teasing her, I said,

"Oh, so you're daring me now. Are you?"

In pretence, I turned to fetch my camera.

"GEOFFREY! You come back here right this very minute, or I'll never forgive you!"

Mother was still half-laughing as she struggled to get her breath.

I laughed, and as I turned back toward Mother, I squatted down and patted my thighs with the flat of my hands and called,

"Here, Beauty. Come on. Good girl."

With one bound, the fat black Labrador jumped off Mother's chest and shot toward me, but obedient Beauty wasn't going anywhere; she just came to a grinding dead-end emergency...

Stop!

The reason was, as instructed, good old Mother was still hanging on to her lead.

I joked,

"At least I have taught you to do something

right."

Still lying on the woodland floor, Mother shouted to me in her most authoritative tone,

"GEOFFREY! Don't just stand there gawping. Please help me up!"

I realised by now Mother was using my name Geoffrey a lot, so I knew she really meant business. With that, I quickly went over and helped her to her feet and said,

"Mum, how on earth did you get yourself into this predicament?"

She replied,

"Beauty was fussing me, and then she got carried away. Before I knew what was happening, she jumped up and knocked me onto my back. The next minute, she was sitting on my chest. The more I shouted, the more Beauty seemed to think it was a game. All my face is wet from where she kept licking me. I was shouting, but no one came to help. I must have been lying here for over thirty minutes. I just couldn't move."

Mother was always prone to just a little bit of

exaggeration, like maybe sometimes trebling it. I estimated it would have been a lot less time with my brief calculation. It was more than likely to assume that she had been lying there with big, fat Beauty on her chest for about five minutes. I have to admit that it was still rather a long time to have a very fat, overweight Labrador pinning you down.

Putting as much sympathy as possible in my voice, I said,

"Are you ok? You're not hurt, are you?"

She snapped,

"Of course, I'm ok. I'm just exhausted from laughing at Beauty."

Mother has always been a very good sport, and out of everyone I've ever known, she was still the first to laugh and see the funny side of things. For sure, that instance was certainly no exception. I think by now, you must be getting the picture that Mother got herself into some unusual predicaments, and she did love to exaggerate ever so slightly. It was and still is part of her nature that everything is twice as big, or twice as small, or twice as disastrous as anything she had ever seen before. So, now you will click on why I have written this next short story.

Edna

In the early days, Kathy and I didn't get too many chances to get away from the business for a holiday. But when we did, Mother stayed and babysat our cottage. She often used to come with her best friend Edna, who was a lovely Welsh lady. Edna was petite and frail and quite a few years older than Mother.

When we were away, I phoned home each evening to check how things were going with Mother and Edna and, of course, the pet hotel. The startling information often sounded quite horrendous with numerous disasters happening to our business. According to Mother, the rapidly mounting problems sounded mind-blowing. So, after a while, or should I say quite a few near-nervous breakdowns, I used to get Kathy to speak to Mother first and check just how the land lay or how things really were. If I had gone on the line first, there would have been so many disasters and catastrophes that you would not believe. It led me to think we would be bankrupt before we returned home. After my phone calls to Mother, it used to take Kathy at least half an hour to calm me down and give me some Mother-de-exaggeration counselling!

On one memorable occasion, I phoned only to find Edna had been helping to walk the dogs from the kennels. I had no idea why, we had plenty of staff, and Edna was most certainly getting on in years.

Apparently, Edna had stepped into a rabbit hole and broken her leg.

'WHAT?'

'Jesus Christ, Edna with a broken leg?'

I was distraught because I knew broken legs could kill old ladies.

Anyway, it turned out toward the end of the telephone conversation that Edna had only nearly broken her leg, yet another of Mother's exaggerations. Missing out the word 'nearly' was an essential part of that initial conversation. After all, there is a vast difference between breaking your leg and nearly breaking your leg.

Over the years, I recall many dramatic telephone conversations with Mother. Such as twenty dogs dying in one week. A slight exaggeration by Geoff this time! Anyway, all these so-called catastrophes just didn't happen as Mother would have led me to believe. Of course, there weren't any so-called disasters at all, but only the regular day-to-day run-of-the-mill events whilst running a busy pet hotel.

So, when Mother stayed in our cottage, we all got wise to her elaborate stories. The staff gave Mother very little information and only what was absolutely necessary. And I emphasise only what was necessary!

I used to take a short time off from skiing to phone during the day and speak to the manager to see if there was anything significant that I should know about. I always phoned Mother on the business line in the evening, not the private line. She would be cheerful on the business line because she would be expecting a customer to be calling, rather than her son or daughter-in-law to whom she could give all the latest 'doom and gloom' news, as we were trying to enjoy ourselves on holiday. Once I heard the cheerful version of Mother's voice, I knew I was on to a winner.

It gave me the chance to say,

"Oh, you sound well and cheerful mum. I gather there are no problems at all, and everything is going well."

So, by then, it would have been too late. Mother was unable to use her dramatic private line voice, with all the 'weight of the world' on her shoulders. But as the saying goes, 'you live and learn'.

Fred

Now, this is an absolute classic!

Another of Mother's walks was with an aged white Bulldog named Fred. Many people do not realise that Bulldogs do not have a very long shelf life. Unfortunately for that breed, every day over six years is a bonus. Fred was six and a half and because of his arthritis accompanied by poor eyesight, he looked to have one foot in the grave. For sure, he was most definitely on borrowed time, but he still enjoyed his walks. With Fred being so old and slow, Mother was the prime candidate to take him. She had loads of patience with him because it took poor old Fred at least four times as long to cover the same distance as the younger, fitter dogs.

One sunny afternoon, Mother was out walking with Fred for a much more extended period than expected, so I decided to investigate.

As I walked briskly along the woodland path, my poor mum was walking toward me, Fred-less.

Also, I could see that she was crying.

This caused me great concern.

I ran up to her and said,

"What on earth is wrong, Mum?"

She sobbed and said,

"Fred's dead!"

"WHAT?"

"Fred's dead!"

With a look of horror on my face, I asked,

"OH! NO! Are you sure?"

"Yes, I'm positive; He just dropped dead like a stone. I tried to revive him, but there was just no response."

'Oh no, I hope she hasn't attempted to give him the kiss of life!'

Well, I certainly didn't fancy a go, as Fred wasn't

particularly that good-looking, and if you can picture what a Bulldog looks like, neither would you. Bulldogs have big fat frog-like mouths with protruding lips, usually accompanied by slimy, slobbery, dribble. Yuk!

With tears flowing, Mother sobbed even more and pointed to where she had left dead Fred, I held her hand, and hastily, we walked over to his dead body.

Dead body?

What dead body?

Dead Fred was nowhere to be seen.

"Are you sure this is the right place, Mum?"

She looked totally bewildered as she gazed around and stammered,

"Well, I think so."

We walked on a little further.

But still no Fred!

I was puzzled,

“Mum, are you sure he was dead?"

“I’m positive he’s dead.”

She sobbed,

“He wasn’t breathing. I even put my ear to his chest and couldn’t hear his heart beating.”

More puzzled I said,

“Perhaps we are in the wrong place.”

We walked on even further.

But still, no dead Fred!

Trying to cheer Mother up, I added a bit of humour and said,

“Surely, he hasn’t gone to heaven already.”

Mother turned around to me, looked me straight in the eye and amazed me as she said,

"Really. Do you think so?"

'I hope she's joking. Surely, she's joking!'

I looked over her shoulder, pointed and said,

"Gone to heaven, gone to heaven. Like the heck he has. He's over there. Look!"

Mother looked to where I was pointing, and sure enough, Fred was most definitely not dead. In fact, he was very much alive, mooching and strolling along at his tortoise-like pace, obviously without a care in the world. For sure, we were extremely thrilled to see him, as I am sure Fred was relieved to know he wasn't dead.

Relieved I said,

"Ok, Mum, no false alarms next time you walk him. My heart can't stand any more frights like this, let alone yours. And we won't mention Fred's!"

Mother retaliated and snapped back grudgingly,

"Don't worry. I'm not walking him again."

I put my arm around her in a bid to soothe her and said,

“Of course, you will. Fred is a lovely dog, and anyway, lightning doesn’t strike twice. Perhaps he over-balanced and toppled over and felt like he needed a little rest.”

I eventually persuaded Mother to walk good old Fred, only because no other member of staff wanted to take him with him being so slow.

Well, everything went well over the next two days until Mother arrived breathless again during the morning dog walking session.

Fred-less?

Mother was distraught and sobbed,

“Fred’s definitely dead now!”

I had a horrible feeling that she could be right this time.

Fred’s owners had informed us when they delivered him that he had been suffering from mild heart attacks and amazingly recovered from them quite quickly, so there would be no urgent need to call the vet. The caring couple had been hanging on all year trying to take a holiday, not wanting to leave poor old Fred with anyone, but in the end, they just felt they had to take a much-needed break. As I have mentioned before, we were quite used to taking in older pets and caring for them as long as the owners were prepared for what could be the worst. Fortunately, we lost very few older pets. But I am afraid we did lose one young one, but that is yet another story. When it occasionally happened with older ones, it was always unfortunate for us and more so for the owners.

Now back to Fred, lying, dying, or dead in the wood.

Showing affection and sympathy, I squeezed Mother's hand and said,

"Come on Mum. Let's go and check the old man out."

I put my arm around Mother's shoulders to console her, and still with me not believing Fred was dead, we walked to where she thought she had left him. Sadly, we eventually found poor old Fred lying in the wood. Unfortunately, Mother was right this time because the poor old lad was as dead as a dodo. There was no sign of life, and there was most certainly no 'kiss-of-life' forthcoming from me. And I sure wasn't going to ask Mother. Because, knowing Mother, she might very well have attempted it!

Poor old Fred was lying flat on his back with his feet and Bulldog nose pointing up toward heaven. He had succumbed about one hundred and twenty yards away from the kennels. I knew Fred was going to be very heavy to move. Do you realise how heavy a Bulldog can be? Well, a fit male could weigh up to fifty-five pounds, but poor old fat Fred had got to be a lot more than that. There was no way I would attempt to carry the poor old lad such a long distance. He would be an absolute solid 'dead weight'. I am sure there's a joke there somewhere. So, I thought it would be a good idea to fetch a wheelbarrow and a hessian sack to cover him up.

I led Mother by her hand back to the kennels with her being so distressed and sobbing. It was always quite shocking to see a dead animal, especially when you had gotten quite attached to them. It was quite apparent that Mother had indeed got quite fond of poor old dead Fred.

As we walked back, I put my arm around her yet again to try and console her.

I said,

"You must remember Mum. He's had a good life. What could be a better way to die than when you have a lovely walk with a lovely lady in beautiful woodland and just keel over peacefully? Not a bad way to go, is it?"

Mother seemed to perk up a little with my kind words, so I continued,

"Mum, the best thing you can do is help with the rest of the dog walking. I'm sure that'll take your mind off things and don't worry. I'll sort poor old Fred out."

I left Mother in the staff room wiping tears from her eyes with my big white hanky and went to get my trusty wheelbarrow, two hessian sacks and more importantly, a strong girl named Hannah. I knew that it would take two of us to lift poor old Fred gently into the wheelbarrow. So, my idea was to roll Fred onto the first hessian sack, lift him into the wheelbarrow, and protect his dignity by covering him up with the other. Having located Hannah, we walked into the wood and rounded the corner where Mother and I had left dead Fred lying.

Guess what?

No dead Fred!

Dead Fred was nowhere to be seen.

Fred had disappeared yet again.

Does this remind you of a story from the Bible?

Has Fred been resurrected?

Hannah gave me a knowing look.

Realizing she thought I was playing a joke, I turned to her and said,

"Honestly, this is definitely where we left him. How many lives has this Bulldog got?"

I am sure Hannah still thought I was joking. I was totally bewildered as I looked around, knowing for sure that this was the exact spot Mother and I had left dead Fred.

'No wonder most of these Bulldogs get called Churchill or Winston. They are indestructible.'

Hannah pointed and shouted,

"THERE HE IS!"

Well, I must say, yet again it was a fantastic relief to see good old Fred wandering toward us on his own little planet with no care in his world, just sniffing and snuffling around as if nothing unusual had happened. When I told Mother the excellent news, she started smiling again. Her tranquil world had returned to normal.

A few days later, Fred's owners turned up to collect him, dead or alive. And thank goodness, he was very much alive this time. They were absolutely thrilled to see him alive and looking so well. I told them all about Fred's two great escapes from the 'Grim Reaper' and how Mother, who loved him to bits, was so relieved he had come back to life.

Fred's owner casually informed me,

"Oh, sorry, Mr Doody, he does that quite often. He's been doing it for a couple of years now, and he is often out cold for ages."

'Oh great, thanks for letting us know; now you are

collecting him!'

If you recall, they only informed us that Fred had mild heart attacks, not drop-dead attacks. But of course, most owners are too afraid to say too much because we might have refused to board their dying dogs. It was very rare for us to decline an ailing dog, whatever its medical condition was.

Anyway, Mother could at least sleep at night, not having the stress of dead Fred on her mind. In fact, he made it to the ripe old age of eight, an outstanding achievement for a Bulldog. I am sure he must have died with a smile on his face, maybe dreaming about his good friend, my Mother.

I just hope they didn't bury the poor old lad alive!

FOOTNOTE

I hope you enjoyed this first book in the series of three.

The second book, besides cats and dogs, features amusing stories about other animals, such as bats, fish, and rats. Plus, a not to be missed nightmare ride in a JCB.

I am sure that some of you would like to know how I got involved in the pet boarding business, or maybe you might want to start one yourself.

Well, you will find out how it all came to pass in book three, the final humorous book in this series.

ACKNOWLEDGEMENT

To my incredible wife Kathy, who has had the patience of a saint to work with me over the years. She painstakingly typed my awful long-hand and helped to revamp it hundreds of times since into this delightful, humorous collection of stories.

My sincere thanks to Mick, who has drawn the amazing caricatures giving the book its very own personality.

I would also like to thank all my family, friends, customers and their pets, of which many are characters in my book.

A special thanks to my managers, Clare, Debbie, Kick, Pat and Erica.

And to all my girls, Amy, Caroline, Charlotte, Gill, Haley, Hannah, Jemma, Jenny, Tracey and other staff that I may have overlooked.

Although all the stories are true, some names have been changed to protect identities.

AUTHOR BIO

Geoff was born in Newport a small historic market town in the county of Shropshire, England. His career ranged from shopkeeper, restaurateur, sales rep, gamekeeper, builder, followed by the pet hotel from where his stories materialised.

The pet hotel/cattery & kennels known as Chetwynd Firs is still situated in an idyllic spot three miles north of Newport just off the A41 highway. Newport is very close to the Staffordshire border, therefore, the business served those two counties, plus Cheshire and a large part of the Midlands. Many of Geoff's customers travelled long distances to use his facilities, and in the summertime, there were hundreds of cats, dogs and customers entering the gates of the establishment. Inevitably a vast number of humorous situations and scenarios arose.

Geoff and Kathy live in Thailand with their three cats Drambuie, Sambuca and Tia Maria.

Printed in Great Britain
by Amazon

40527808R00215